RESEARCHING RACE AND SOCIAL JUSTICE IN EDUCATION:
ESSAYS IN HONOUR OF
BARRY TROYNA

ek Loan

last date shown

1858560837

RESEARCHING RACE AND SOCIAL JUSTICE IN EDUCATION: ESSAYS IN HONOUR OF BARRY TROYNA

EDITED BY PAT SIKES AND FAZAL RIZVI

Trentham Books

First published in 1997 by Trentham Books Limited

Trentham Books Limited
Westview House
734 London Road
Oakhill
Stoke on Trent
Staffordshire
England ST4 5NP

British Cataloguing in Publication Data

A catalogue record for this book is available from the British Library
ISBN: 1 85856 083 7

Designed and typeset by Trentham Print Design Ltd., Chester
and printed in Great Britain by The Cromwell Press Ltd., Wiltshire

ACKNOWLEDGEMENTS

We would like to thank friends and colleagues who have helped in the preparation of this festschrift: John Eggleston, Managing Director of Trentham Books for supporting the project; the authors for their enthusiastic and helpful contributions; Donna Jay, Ruth Arber and Janine McAlpine for editorial help; OLW; and Robyn Sikes-Sheard for art work.

TABLE OF CONTENTS

INTRODUCTION
BARRY TROYNA: A LIFE RECALLED
Pat Sikes and Fazal Rizvi

BARRY STEPHEN TROYNA
6th September 1951-9th February 1996

In England, and in the field of educational studies, festschrifts compiled in honour of, and in tribute to, a person's work and life are rare. There are many reasons for why this is, although embarrassment of various kinds tends to play a key role. There may be embarrassment at raising someone up in this way, embarrassment because we are unsure about their 'qualifications' for this type of treatment, embarrassment about the timing of such a volume, embarrassment about revealing our assessment of and feelings for a person, and so on. Whether as readers or contributors we are just not used to this sort of thing and we are not sure of how to approach it. Most of the people who have written for this collection commented on what a painfully difficult experience it had been not only because of the way it emphasised that Barry Troyna is no longer with us but also because few of us have any experience of writing for a festschrift. Acknowledging how hard it was for them, we would like to record our thanks right at the start.

We undertook to put this Festschrift together because it is our view that Barry made an important contribution to thinking about 'race' and racism and about researching social justice issues in the school context and, thereby, had a positive influence on the experiences of many young people and teachers. He is, therefore, a worthy candidate for commemoration of this kind. We also did it because during Barry's long illness we had often talked about such a project. Our view was that that while a festschrift for someone so young might cause some eyebrows to raise, it would be valuable not only by recognising Barry's enormous contribution to the field but also in providing an account of how an academic life can link up productively with the various sites of educational practice, and in showing how academic work 'travels', circulates and becomes influential. From Barry's own point of view, he agreed to the project not out of any desire for self-aggrandisement but, rather as an attempt to challenge and come to terms with what was happening to him and with what he knew was going to happen. With hindsight, we also think that he saw it as a strategy for helping some of his friends and colleagues to cope too.

Death has far-reaching consequences, changing and impacting upon people in many different ways. Those of us who knew Barry know only too well what his death has meant for us in a personal sense. Writing this more than a year after the event, we continue to find it incredible that he is dead and, paradoxically, that there are people in the world who don't know that he is. Every week post arrives for him containing requests to examine PhDs, read papers, speak at conferences, provide information about his work, and so on. But then, why should people know? Barry's writings are out there in the public domain in the same way that they always were and his death makes no difference to their accessibility. It can be seen to make a difference to their meaning though, in that he is not here to assess, to explain, to reinterpret, develop or change his thinking in response to changing circumstances or altered insights and perceptions. In the future others will no doubt, deliberately or unconsciously, do these things as they refer to, question and build on what he had to say. This book begins the process of recognising what he did and considering the legacies that he left. With this as our purpose, the starting point has to be with the man himself.

Inevitably any biography that we might offer will be partial, biased and, in the context of this book, almost insultingly brief. In any circumstances it is difficult to know what to include in a life story because, to a large degree, what different people want to know depends upon their interests and concerns. It is never possible to capture a total life in words and communicating a sense of what Barry was like for people who didn't know him isn't easy. He was a vital man, alert and energetic, both physically and mentally. He worked and played as hard as he could, putting all of his resources into whatever he was involved in. He could be tremendously enthusiastic and many colleagues and students would come away after talking to him about a potential piece of work feeling fired up and excited at the prospect of getting started. He was an enabler and a sponsor to many young researchers and he could provoke extreme loyalty. Indeed it is probably true that people either 'loved' him or 'hated' him: it was difficult to be indifferent because in some ways he was a larger than life character. Some measure of how he did affect people can be gathered from the vast number of cards and letters which arrived from all over the world when he first became ill. He himself was overwhelmed and extremely touched by this and particularly by the good wishes he received from people he had only met in the briefest manner.

Looking back on his life, the suggestion that Barry was a complex and contradictory person appears perfectly apt. As much as he was kind and supportive, he could also be appallingly unkind, cutting, hurtful, sarcastic, selfish and tyrannical. He was almost always passionately committed to his point of view about anything and could at times be unjustifiably scathing about any other position. He often got into heated arguments. He had a passion for discussions about all kinds of things from 'post-modern bollocks' to the beauty of a Glen Hoddle goal for his beloved Tottenham Hotspurs. This account should not be taken to suggest however, that Barry was somehow inflexible or dogmatic. But it does indicate that he would always need a great deal of convincing before he would consider changing his mind. He once confided that views held with passion should not simply be abandoned for the sake of some academic fashion.

Barry loved Tottenham Hotspurs football team with his whole heart. He was keen on other sports, especially tennis and rugby. He liked music and reading and travel. He enjoyed a hectic social life and he had friends from a variety of backgrounds. He could be great fun to be with because he was amusing, cheeky, challenging and provocative. Twenty-two months before he died he had married Sally who brought him security and, as he once put it, a sense of home to go back to. Things were looking good for him, and then he became ill.

The cancer was remorseless and, even in the brief period of remission that he had, never really lost its hold. Like Barry himself, 'it' was tenacious and aggressive and finally 'it' hijacked his life.

Illness is a very personal experience but we mention it not least because if Barry hadn't been ill this book would not have happened. It is also the case that it is impossible to separate out the personal from the professional aspects of any life. At a fundamental level, Barry's illness had implications for his attitude towards his work, and as a researcher with an active interest in life history methodology he was not reticent about acknowledging and making explicit links between the various components of his life.

Indeed, in the Preface to his book, *Racism and Education* (1993), Barry offered an autobiographical account to explain how and why he had come to devote most of his working life to studying issues and aspects of 'race' and education. As he saw it, his commitment to social justice was inextricably related to fundamental and salient experiences within his life.

He was the son of Jewish parents and was born and brought up in Tottenham. During the 1950s and 1960s this area of North London became home to large numbers of Afro-Caribbean immigrants whose children went to the same schools as Barry did. He 'witnessed the racist abuse (they) experienced within and beyond the school gates' (1993, p.viii) and, for his own part, 'experienced similar forms of harassment, especially from the racist and anti-Semitic activities of the British Movement and National Front' (ibid).

Although he was academically able, passed the eleven plus and gained a place at Tottenham Grammar School (where Spurs was founded), in terms of '0' and 'A' levels results, his school career was not outstanding. He attributed his relatively poor results to an overwhelming passion for football, and to the elitist attitudes and values of teachers which were, to some extent, exacerbated by the reorganisation of the school from selective to comprehensive. Yet despite, or because of, experiences of school which were 'less than gratifying' (ibid, p.vi), he went on to teacher training college in Nottingham, chosen, so he claimed, solely because it was the birthplace of his great literary hero, D.H. Lawrence!

While he had ended up on a teaching course largely because his A levels weren't good enough for university, Barry was motivated to teach because, in common with many others, especially others of his particular generation, he had a lot of faith in the power of education as a means to achieving social justice. While he retained that faith for the rest of his life, he shared Apple's view that 'the social democratic goal of expanding equality of opportunity ... has lost much of its political potency and its ability to mobilise people' (Quoted in Troyna, 1994, p.2), acknowledging that political discourses, events and trends in the 1980s and 90s led to other projects gaining the ascendancy. His experiences at college were not, however, that much better than or different from what had happened at school. He was always uncomfortable with the elitist values he encountered in lecturers and other students. Undeterred he graduated and got a job in a 'community' comprehensive school.

Disillusionment over the gap between the rhetoric and the reality of the comprehensive ideal as he saw it being enacted at that school and in others like it, led to him leaving and taking up postgraduate study at the Centre for Mass Communications Research at Leicester University. His research focused on reggae and Rastafari in the lives of Afro-Caribbean boys in Britain. As well as his academic interest in the topic, this work not only gave him an excuse to listen to music, which, as we have noted, was one of his great enthusiasms but it also constituted the beginning of his commitment to antiracism. He was able to combine his academic and personal interests, though it was not till much later that he was able to admit that the personal could not easily be separated from the theoretical positions one favoured.

Although it had been his intention to return to school-teaching when he had completed his dissertation, he never did. Research projects followed at the ESRC Research Unit on Ethnic Relations at Aston and Warwick (now the Centre for Research on Ethnic Relations), then came a readership at what was then Sunderland Polytechnic, and finally he returned to Warwick as a Lecturer in the Social Aspects of Education in the Department of Education in 1988. Here he continued to conduct research into aspects of 'race' and education but, over time, became increasingly interested in issues associated with educational policy, research methodology and, in particular, with questions around the 'empowering' and 'emancipatory' potential of research. He was on the editorial boards of a number of journals and was especially proud to be editor of the British Education Research Journal. In 1991 he was awarded a D.Litt by Nottingham University in recognition of his published works.

Whilst at Warwick Barry did a fair amount of travelling, lecturing, teaching and speaking at conferences overseas. He travelled extensively through the United States, Canada, Germany, Italy, Spain, New Zealand and of course Australia, where his work was received with especial acclaim. Indeed at one time he was thinking of moving there permanently. Why his work was so well received in Australia is a question one can only speculate about. He was rather a techniphobe, and was terrified for many years, of using a word processor in case he lost his work. However, getting connected up to e-mail was a joy to him because it enabled him to correspond with friends and colleagues throughout the world.

A couple of months before he died Barry was awarded a personal Chair at Warwick. When the Vice Chancellor visited the hospital to give him the news of his promotion he was very weak and it seemed that his death was only hours away. Within a very short time though, he was sitting up and, characteristically, ordering everyone around, demanding that his friends and colleagues should be told and generally making plans for what he was going to do when he got back to the university. In the event, he did manage to go to work as a professor for a week or two. This cost him an enormous effort but, at the same time, gave him immense pleasure.

As a teacher, lecturer and researcher Barry's primary concern was to question, and to encourage students to question, conventional wisdoms and taken for granted assumptions. He was an exciting, inspirational, provocative and encouraging teacher, not least because he was down to earth and was always able to give practical and real examples to illustrate theory. This ability was the result of his concern to get into schools and to work with youngsters in class-rooms which he did, both in his capacity as governor of a local primary school, and in the various research projects he was involved in. Because he did have this practical involvement in schools and because his style of writing was clear and straightforward, his work didn't just reach the academic community: he was widely read by teachers, many of whom took up and put his ideas around issues of racial equality and social justice into practice It may sound a grandiose claim but it is our view that few researchers or academics have made a difference to children's lives the way Barry Troyna's efforts did. We will now move on to assess that work in a wider context.

As we have already noted, Barry's earliest research was on reggae and Rastafari in the lives of Afro-Caribbean boys in Britain. In the mid 1970s, this focus on popular culture was indeed pioneering. Few educational researchers at that time studied popular black culture in order to understand issues of ethnic identity and racism in Britain. In that work, Barry tied questions of ethnicity to issues of class in ways that were not dissimilar to the ways that the researchers at the Centre for Contemporary Cultural Studies (CCCS) in Birmingham were seeking to do. He used Gramsci's idea of hegemony to provide an account of the educational experiences and aspirations of the Afro-Caribbean boys he studied. He showed that identity for these boys was constructed in a context of a politics of resistance to the dominant hegemonic forms of culture in expressions in which reggae and Rastafari played a significant role.

This research demonstrated an interest that Barry had throughout his career in questions of masculinity, long before they became fashionable. Barry's work has often been criticised for its gender blindness but his view was that he could best utilise the emerging theoretical resources of feminism by looking at his own masculinity. As well, he was deeply suspicious of the way some male writers highjacked feminist issues for their own careerist interests.

In the early 1980s Barry's research interest shifted to address more directly the issues of racism. He was convinced that the term 'racism' was a contested one and that debates over its meaning always involved questions of how it was best represented, how its forms changed and how generalisable were its expressions. He believed that these were not simply terminological issues but were issues that were inherently practical and political, concerned with questions of not only knowledge and power but also desire and hope.

Much of his work was therefore directed at showing that it was impossible to research questions of 'race' relations in a neutral or objective manner. He rejected the claim of traditional sociology to provide an authoritative account of how things actually were. He believed instead that such claims to knowledge were always linked to certain entrenched ruling interests. The study of racism, he believed, involved 'seeing' the world against the understanding the researcher had of its salience. The researcher could not therefore, simply stand apart from the social and political relations that constituted the research processes and was unavoidably implicated in the dynamics of racial structuring. In seeking knowledge about racism the researcher entered into a social relation with those who were being researched.

In this way, Barry increasingly began to recognise that the personal could not be divorced from the research processes. Researching racism involved an attempt to understand the practices of representation and the way they were organised, persisted and changed. This, at least in part, explains the way his political commitment to social justice was informed by his epistemological position, as well as his theorising of the process of racialisation. Borrowing from Reeve (1983), he used the idea of racialisation extensively, long before postcolonial theorists like Goldberg (1993) discovered it. He saw it as a useful concept in examining the policy discourses of multiculturalism.

It was not until the mid 1980s that Barry began to investigate the policy processes surrounding the development, dissemination and legitimation of multicultural education. He viewed multiculturalism as a hegemonic strategy by which the State sought to manage issues of race relations and problems of racism in Britain. Multiculturalism was a compromise formation between the State's desire to ensure social conditions necessary for capital accumulation on the one hand and the management of popular demands for justice by the immigrant communities on the other.

In examining policy issues Barry rejected the traditional view of policy analysis as a systematic study of the processes of decision-making as they related to the issues of implementation and program evaluation, but saw it instead as an exploration of how particular policy formulations were put on the agenda, and how they were contested and re-articulated at the local levels. For him, an examination of policies required an assessment of the issues of power and control. As a result, much of his policy analysis work was focused on the ways in which school and local education authorities interpreted multiculturalism. His concern was to challenge some of the liberal assumptions implicit in a multicultural approach and to posit, in its place, an antiracism that was based on transforming existing relations of social and economic power.

Barry was fond of saying that the task of the social scientist was not only in 'taking things apart' but also in presenting valuable and ethically justifiable alternatives to mainstream policy solutions. He had always thought that multiculturalism had become part of a slogan system and that, as a term, it incorporated a set of beliefs that reproduced social inequalities in British society. Antiracism on the other hand suggested a much more political response to the problems faced by the immigrant communities in Britain. He argued that multiculturalism and antiracism represented two irreconcilable perspectives. He argued that 'they imply a very different idea of the nature and processes of racism which, in turn, promote the development of different frameworks within which specific priorities of action are embedded' (1987, p.311). It is this contrast that lies at the centre of much of Barry's research career. Indeed he has become most clearly identified by it.

Much to the surprise of many of his colleagues and friends, Barry insisted on maintaining the distinction between multiculturalism and antiracism until the end. He was, of course, much criticised for this dualism. For him, however, the distinction was not so much a conceptual as a political one. Antiracism highlighted an oppositional politics that set it apart from the liberal individualism within which multiculturalism was embedded. Indeed in many ways Barry was an anti-dualist thinker so it is ironic indeed that he is remembered by many as having had what they saw as a blind spot when it came to the 'distinction'.

For Barry, while values and commitments to social justice remained fundamental, he saw the means to bring about social justice as inherently dynamic. He insisted upon the need to think prag-matically and politically about responses to the problems of racism. Indeed in view of his convictions that no universal characterisation of the nature of racism was possible; that the representations and practices of racism were continually changing, being challenged, interrupted and deconstructed; and that racism was a pre-eminently socio-historical concept, then the theoretical distinction between multiculturalism and antiracism makes no sense at all. If processes of racialisation are continually changing, then so must our responses to it.

In Thatcherite Britain many of Barry's ideas became a symbol of what the British state did not like about not only sociology but especially, a politically committed antiracism. There were many attempts in the popular media to discredit Troyna personally. When he was about to embark on his Racism in Children's Lives Project with Richard Hatcher, newspapers like the *Daily Mail* and the *Sun* ran editorials ridiculing efforts to show issues of racism to be relevant to the education of young children, and saw the project as representing everything that was wrong with 'the loony left'.

Barry felt that a response to this Conservative attack was to understand its premises and to devise practical strategies of antiracism that got around some of the impediments it clearly represented. In his book with Bruce Carrington, *Education, Racism and Reform* (1990), Barry explored what room for practical manoeuvre there might have been left for an antiracist education in a political context that was dominated by the New Right, and the systematic attack it had mounted on the capacity of local authorities to support equal opportunity initiatives. He concluded that in such a context only a defensive struggle was possible.

Part of this recognition involved him in exploring ways in which young children understood and worked with racialised ideas. The upshot of this research was to identify the complex ways in which practices of racism were linked to broader political and institutional contexts. This research also led Barry to explore the world of teachers' work and to look at how, in everyday practices, they could challenge racist vocabulary, social practices and organisations. During the last two years of his life, Barry was increasingly fascinated by two new areas of research: postcolonial writings, and in particular the notions of 'racialised silence' and 'whiteness' in the work of Toni Morrison and 'recognition' theories of social justice as put forward by feminist philosophers such as Iris Marion Young and Nancy Fraser.

Recent work with both children and teachers brought Barry back full circle to his original training as a teacher. Towards the end of his life he spent a great deal of time in schools both as a visitor and as a governor of a local primary school in Coventry. He felt that the world of policy and academic theorising did not always understand the way policies impacted on teachers' lives, and that such an understanding was essential for an effective politics of antiracism. Increasingly, ethical and interpersonal concerns began to feature more prominently in Barry's work, replacing a preoccupation with issues of structures and institutions that had marked his earlier work.

Just before he died he confided that his had been a full academic life but that he had barely begun to scratch the surface of the issues that remained for him to understand.

This collection thus has two purposes: to understand Barry and his work, and to extend his contribution to our understanding of the complexities of racial politics in education. As we have already said, we talked with Barry about this festschrift extensively. After initial hesitation, he was enthusiastic and was pleased to have us work on it. He was very close to Pat, not least because her office at the University of Warwick was next to his, but also because they taught courses together and regularly talked about issues of education, politics and research. He also thought that Fazal was in a good position to represent the international dimension of Barry's work. Fazal and Barry had become good friends following Barry's regular visits to Australia. They 'hung out' together at conferences and worked on a number of projects.

Characteristically, Barry had clear ideas about who should be asked to contribute in order to represent various stages and aspects of his career. A list of names was written down when he discovered that he was terminally ill and then put away in a drawer. At that stage, naively perhaps, there seemed to be room for optimism and death was still very much an abstract notion. Then when Barry died there was that abysmal sense of emptiness that most people who have been bereaved will recognise. Nothing was right any more and it was hard to find the energy to do very much. Sally organised a wonderful funeral which celebrated Barry's life, his enthusiasms and his values. There was music by Frankie Goes To Hollywood, an account of his work by John Eggleston, Kaddish, performed by his father and brother by the graveside, and an enormous wreath in the form of Spurs' crest.

Obituaries and tributes appeared in the educational press, in academic journals and in national newspapers. We made an half-hearted and unsuccessful attempt to do something about the festschrift but, although we were desperately keen to honour our promise, we knew that the time wasn't really right. Then Carol

Vincent took on the responsibility of organising a memorial seminar for Barry at the 1996 British Educational Research Association conference, some six months after his death.

The seminar took the form of eight brief and quite personal accounts of Barry and of his work. The event was an emotional affair and, in many ways served as a valuable part of the grieving process for someone who had died so prematurely. Following the seminar a number of people expressed the view that it would be appropriate to have a more permanent record and to have what had been said in print. It was only then that it seemed as right a time as any to go ahead with the festschrift and consequently we contacted the people on the list Barry and the two of us had drawn up, eighteen months before. Almost everyone we approached was honoured to participate in the project, and their co-operation has demonstrated once again the high regard in which Barry was held by his friends and colleagues. It was Barry himself who had suggested that Trentham Books, the publishing company founded by John Eggleston, might consider publishing the Festschrift. Not surprisingly Trentham were as keen to participate as the contributors, who all agreed that all royalties accruing from the book would be sent to the Radio-therapy Unit at Walsgrave Hospital in Coventry, where Barry was cared for throughout his illness and where he eventually died.

In a letter sent to contributors we suggested that in their writing they: 'may want to focus on (their) understanding of Barry's work, his contribution to academic and political work, (their) view of the ways in which (their) own work has been inspired by this contribution and the manner in which (they) think the debates about which he wrote are now shaping up'. Some people found this easier to do than others did. As we noted earlier, the majority of the contributors talked about how hard it was to write anything at all. This was frequently due to the pain they felt as a result of his death but some also commented on how difficult it is to write about a person who isn't here to answer back. A number of the contributors stressed that they were unable to write from anything other than a personal perspective: they felt that they had to bring in memories and refer to incidents and personal quirks in order to capture the essence of Barry as they knew him. Writing for a book of this kind was a unique experience and people had to find their own way through.

The organisation of the papers in this collection moves from largely personal accounts to papers which assess more broadly the significance of Barry's academic ideas to the on-going politics of equal opportunities in education. The first paper by Carol Vincent points to some of the dilemmas that she had as a former doctoral student of Barry. The papers by Sally Tomlinson and David Halpin assess Barry's ethical and political commitments, and the ways they informed his views on educational research.

In the next two papers, Jean Rudduck writes in appreciation of Barry's work for the British Educational Research Association and Gaby Weiner discusses his editorship of the Association's journal and some of his views on academic publishing. The paper by Sandra Shipton describes Barry's work as a governor of the primary school at which she is the Headteacher. The next paper has a very different form: in it Ivor Goodson makes some preliminary remarks about Barry as a researcher. These remarks are followed by an edited text of a conversation Barry and Ivor had in 1995 about life-history as a research methodology in education. The papers by Vicki Crowley and Roger Dale are written from Australia and New Zealand, assessing how Barry's theories 'travelled' internationally.

In the next paper, Bob Lingard examines the ways in which Barry theorised the state. This paper is followed by an essay by John Rex which reassesses the debates surrounding the contrast between multiculturalism and antiracism. And finally, Richard Hatcher provides an overview of Barry's work, speculating on its relevance for thinking about social justice issues in education under the new Labour government in Britain.

Almost all of Barry's academic work was done under successive Conservative governments hostile to the values he fought so hard to promote. It is indeed ironic that we are writing this Introduction to a festschrift in his honour soon after the Conservatives have been electorally defeated. Barry would have enjoyed this sense of timing. But there is no guarantee that the political values of justice and democracy in education for which he fought so hard will get a better reception by the new government. Barry's advice to us all would have been to continue the struggle.

References

Goldberg, D. (1993) *Racist Culture, Philosophy and the Politics of Meaning*, Oxford, Blackwell

Reeve, F. (1983) *British Racial Discourse: A Study of British Political Discourse About Race and Race Related Matters*, Cambridge, Cambridge University Press

Troyna, B. (1987) 'Beyond Multiculturalism: Towards the Enactment of Antiracist Education in Policy, Provision and Pedagogy', *Oxford Review of Education* Vol 13, No 3 (Reprinted in S. Allen and M. Macey (Eds.) *Race and Social Policy,* ESRC, London (1988) pp.307-320

Troyna, B. and Carrington, S. (1990) *Education, Racism and Reform*, London, Routledge

Troyna, B. (1992) *Racism in Children's Lives*, London, Routledge

Troyna, B. (1993) *Racism and Education*, Buckingham, Open University

Troyna, B. (1994) 'Reforms, Research and Being Reflexive About being Reflective', in Halpin, D. and Troyna, B. (Eds.) *Researching Education Policy: Ethical and Methodological Issues,* London, Falmer

1

BARRY TROYNA: A DISSENTING VOICE?

Carol Vincent

During the planning stages of this festschrift, the editors sent out a letter to the contributors which set out its scope and direction. It stated,

> As we will be including in our own introduction a great many biographical details, there is no need for you to do this as well. It is the relationship of your work to [Barry's] that we would like emphasised. We are looking for chapters that have an academic orientation, that push Barry's work into new directions, rather than something that reads like an obituary.

My initial reaction was, I must admit, one of dismay. They were asking for a piece I felt far from equipped to write. In saying this, I intend no criticism of Pat and Fazal's plans. In their place as editor, I think I would have identified the same focus as being most appropriate, and written a similar letter. However, I was not in their place, nor writing from their viewpoint, and I felt unequal to the task with which I was presented. My reluctance to engage with it may seem baffling, at least, it initially struck me as being so. I knew Barry for seven years. I was his PhD student, and students, through a combination of opportunity and strategy, usually read and use most of their supervisor's work. More recently Barry and I had begun to write jointly. We had several plans for future research and had, before his death, begun to put these into practice. On these indices, I appear ideally placed to comment on my understanding of Barry's work, and the way in which my own work has developed as a result of his.

Part of the constraints I felt were due, I think, to the nature of public tributes. Tributes take the form of collections of 'stories' which when put together appear to 'sum up' an individual and his/her work. Yet this is clearly impossible. No one written or spoken piece or series of pieces can hope to capture the complexity and entirety of an individual's intellectual, personal and (in Barry's case) Spurs-supporting, life. I know that neither the editors nor the contributors to this volume would claim that they are embarked on a definitive enterprise. They would, I guess, describe their aims as attempting to present illuminating, but partial, insights into Barry's contribution to academic writing and research. Their accounts stress the dynamism of Barry's work, the enduring nature of his ideas as others take up, engage with, and develop them in their own way and in their own contexts. However, my point is that the very existence of a festschrift, an obituary, or a spoken tribute, or any of these forms *implicitly* suggest finality, closure, conclusiveness. As such the responsibility of contributing to them becomes overwhelming – every word seems to set itself in stone. How to comment on someone's work, to engage in a dialogue with them about issues at the centre of their intellectual life, when they cannot respond, cannot question your assertions or interpretations? How to continue to be a reader when the writer is dead?

The other difficulty I have with public tributes is the way in which they threaten the boundaries between the public and the private, as we are generally required to maintain them. The professional imperatives of a coherent, detached narrative are endangered by the personal experience of bereavement. A common response seems to be to regulate the language deemed acceptable for use. Not the words so much, because to talk of the loss and tragedy and waste of someone dying, especially someone as young as Barry, is generally deemed acceptable. But the tone, the appropriate public tone is constrained, inhibited: so that one can speak of loss, but not in a way that suggests the pain, grief, anger or panic that goes with it. Another, and related, way of coping with this blurring of the public and the private is to attempt to disentangle the two, to extract the former, whilst marginalising the latter: to focus on the professional.

After all, conceptual and intellectual differences, inconsistencies, and obscurities are much more easily dealt with than their personal equivalents.

With these half-formed thoughts in my mind, I read Patricia Duncker's (1996) novel *Hallucinating Foucault*. The story is a complex and absorbing one, and I shall draw out only the bare bones of the narrative. It revolves around a writer of fiction, Paul Michel, who is certified insane, and the reader, a student studying his work, who seeks him out. One of the central themes of the book is the relationship between reader and writer. Michel is a contemporary of the French philosopher, Foucault, and the student finds letters the novelist wrote to Foucault; letters written but never sent, in which Michel talks about the bond between the writer and reader.

> My relationship with you is intense because it is addressed every day, through all my working hours... I clear a space to write for you, to you, against you. You are the measure of my abilities...I search for you through the spiral of all my sentences. I throw out whole pages of manuscript because I cannot find you in them. I search for you in small details, in the shape of my verbs, the quality of my phrases...You are the glove that I find on the floor, the daily challenge I take up. You are the reader for whom I write (Dunker, 1996, pp.73-4).

Paul Michel did not know Foucault: he presents theirs as a relationship which existed through their work:

> You [*i.e. one*] are always listening, I think, when you write, for the voice which answers. However oblique the reply may be. Foucault never attempted to contact me. He did something far more frightening, provocative, profound. He wrote back in his published work (*ibid.*, p.152, *my addition*)

At the end of the book, Paul Michel dies. A letter written for the student to Michel claims 'I was your reader too. He [*Foucault*] was not your only reader'.

So absorbed was I by this point that I began to argue with the text. The book describes the student's developing relationship with Paul Michel. Therefore, I reasoned, the student could not be the novelist's reader in the same sense that Foucault was. The anonymity of the relationship between Foucault and Paul Michel, its hallucinatory quality, is essential to the connection Michel feels. A personal relationship with the accompanying day to day interactions, exchanges and trivia that constitute any and every friendship, disrupts the purity of an approach to the text which is unencumbered by any of these things. The stuff of friendship interferes with, and alters any engagement with the written word. The text no longer stands alone or in relation only to other texts, but is caught within the 'fuzzy reality' (Wellman *et al*, 1988) of friendship. A reading of the text is then interwoven with the reader's understandings and interpretations of the writer; understandings not based on the written word alone but on a whole range of apparently extraneous events, conversations, arguments and agreements. This may appear productive, inciting richer and more informed readings. But in this particular case, I find my thoughts impeded and blocked. In short, what I am trying to say, in this rather tortuous fashion, is that between myself and my ability to comment on or assess Barry's work in any way, are my memories of Barry. Perhaps it can't be any other way. For my point holds good, I think, in a wider context than that of one particular friendship. The apparently austere, impersonal academic world with its scholarly concerns and manners is, of course, a highly social world. It is both fractured and sustained by friendships, rivalries, collaborations, disputations, insecurities and confidences. Yet we often choose to overlook, to ignore or disguise the clamorous nature of our social interactions, as if the texts we comment on can be abstracted, and as if the ideas stand alone, independent of their originators.

However, this type of response is undoubtedly a shirking of responsibility. My responsibility to fulfil my agreement with Pat and Fazal to contribute a chapter to this volume, and also, and more fundamentally, a shirking of my debt to Barry. Offering the above account (which Barry may well have seen as a piece of indulgence, game-playing, or in his words 'post-modern bollocks') seems a poor return for the time, energy and commitment he expended on me and my work over the last seven years. So I will start again, marshal my thoughts, and attempt to describe, first of all the example he set as an academic, and second to focus on some of his work on education policy with which I was most closely concerned.

There were, I think, five features of Barry's academic identity which were most apparent to me. First of all, his constant questioning, the taking up of a different stance, of asking 'what is really going on?' and 'how come?' (Troyna, 1994a). Second, and connected to this, was his concern with reflexivity, with ensuring that 'the technicalities of research are no longer artificially detached from the political, ethical and social arena' (Troyna, 1994b p.6). In line with his questioning, dissenting approach, the chapter in which that last quotation appears, subjects the concept of reflexivity to a detailed scrutiny. The third identifying aspect was Barry's writing style. He wrote with confidence, certainty, and clarity. Deconstruction involved reconstruction. Whilst he was concerned to 'question... mainstream boundaries and categories' (Griffiths and Troyna, 1995, p.xx), he was also concerned to 're-draw' them (ibid.), even if only temporarily. The fourth feature was his concern with theory. He would, I think, have agreed with Stephen Ball that,

> Theory provides the possibility of... a language which is not caught up with the assumptions and inscriptions of policy-makers or the immediacy of practice... It offers a potential location outside the prevailing discourses of policy and a way of struggling against 'incorporation' (1997)

As he took part in debates around education policy studies, Barry argued for the broadening of the dominant field of reference for those working within the genre. Feminist and antiracist texts which dealt with concepts of the state, or sought to deconstruct terms which were routinely referred to in the educational discourses of Conservative reform (e.g. 'empowerment') should be, he argued, accorded a central place in the frames of reference employed by policy sociologists (Troyna, 1994a).

His fifth concern was that political activity should not get sidelined by theoretical game-playing. This anxiety informed his early distrust of many strands of postmodernist theorising, and led him to agree with Beverley Skeggs when she argued,

> Any account of responses to education needs to recognise that other forces may have a greater influence than the education system itself. We do need to be careful however, postmodernism may seduce us into competitive gamesmanship; it may stop us asking certain questions, it may lead us into political inaction and despair (1991. p.266)

Thus Barry argued consistently for the integration of critical academic comment with political action; 'deconstructing the obvious' should provide the 'launch pad' rather than the 'destination' for the research enterprise' (Troyna, 1994a p.82). The aim of critical social research should be to seek to 'identify those elements which have the potential to change or resist the 'social reality' as it is articulated through current educational reforms' (*ibid.*)

This particular concern informed his persistent interest in the activities, developments and conflicts focused around the local state. He theorised local education authorities (LEAs) as 'sites of struggle'. In this view, LEAs are arenas in which competing demands and interests – those of parents, teachers, administrators, politicians and local community groups are acted out. This is not to suggest that Barry subscribed to pluralism, a view which argues that competing interest groups meet on a level playing field (Troyna, 1993). On the contrary, the process of policy formulation and implementation is a complex one, involving 'a plurality of discourses and discursive sites, a plurality of positions and perspectives from which to speak. Of course, not all of these have equal authority. Yet conflict and contestation are part of the story' (Fraser, 1992: 53-4)

The extent to which local disputes are framed and controlled by material and ideological developments taking place on national and international stages was a topic Barry frequently discussed (e.g.

Hatcher and Troyna, 1994), but on which he had yet to reach conclusions he found wholly satisfactory. Although he did not subscribe to interpretations of the state which saw it as monolithic and homogeneous, his analyses tended to emphasise central state power. This involved positioning the state centre stage, and seeing structural constraints as having a 'profound impact' on local actors. However, 'a degree of indeterminacy exists, a function of specific local and conjectural circumstances of which differential political and social mobilisation is a crucial variable,' (1994a p.76). In exploring this degree of indeterminacy, the 'space' for local agency and activity, Barry focused increasingly on groups organising within civil society. His interest in relationships between black groups mobilising around racial equality issues and the local state was long-standing (e.g. Troyna and Williams, 1986; Troyna and Carrington, 1990). His focus tended to be the relationship of such groups to and within the local state, and, in particular, the degree of influence they could exercise on policy formulation. This continued analytical interest in the local led to an emphasis on the formation of alliances between heterogeneous interest groups and communities, both within and beyond the sphere of the local state (Troyna and Vincent, 1995; 1996). Two recent papers seek to expand and illustrate these ideas,

> Dawn Oliver refers to 'multiple citizenships' (1991 p.162)... [which] she defines as a sense of belonging to more than one community; an acknowledgement that every individual has links with several social communities; links which result from the interaction of ethnicity, gender and class variables. Her analysis demands that to enhance its effectiveness and relevance, the local state must be prepared to engage in participatory initiatives accessible to all sectors of the local population. For it is in such a setting where the local state demonstrates its concern to address issues raised by heterogeneous communities that we see the greatest potential for the pursuit of social justice issues in education, (Troyna and Vincent, 1995 p.163)

The second quotation is from a jointly written chapter, published after Barry's death, in which we concluded with a similar line of argument. Writing about the collective endeavours of parents' groups active around special education issues, we argued that these fragile forms of organisation,

> Foreshadow the emergence of more effective and co-ordinated attempts to subvert the 'ideology of expertism'. This would not be entirely without precedent as our discussion of racial equality initiatives in the local state testifies. Furthermore, as we noted earlier, the local state is a 'site of struggle' and in these circumstances there remains the potential for closer alliances between professionals, parents and their children in attempts to challenge the hegemonic status of 'the ideology of expertism' . This scenario presumes a 'dynamic as opposed to deterministic relationship between different social interests' (Armstrong, 1995 p.126) which, in this context, refers to professional and lay interpretations of how alternative forms of social justice might be advanced through special education. For some this might seem a forlorn expectation, but we suggest that to think otherwise is to submit to political quiescence and the language of defeatism (Troyna and Vincent, 1996 p.142).

Following on from this, my own interests currently lie in further exploring the actions and activities, the possibilities and problems for groups and organisations within civil society, whose concern is to intervene in educational processes and institutions. In this, I have clearly been influenced by Barry's own agenda.

However, the balance of interests in his own work was shifting more towards methodology, and a consideration of the ways in which research methods could ascribe different amounts of power to various groups involved in research. This led to his interest in 'empowerment' and emancipatory research (Troyna, 1994, 1994a, 1994b). His immediate plans were to address the critique contained within Foster *et al's Constructing Educational Inequality* (1996). This volume focuses on several qualitative researchers (including Barry himself) whose work carefully explores and delineates the educational processes which serve to marginalise particular groups of students. Barry found the critique put forward by Foster and his colleagues unconvincing and unreflexive, and was looking forward to constructing a rebuttal.

So I conclude by noting that Barry's academic work stood at a cross-roads. This is a fitting image, one which serves to integrate the personal and professional themes running through this chapter, in line with my earlier argument that they cannot be separated. For a cross-roads is a location which offers new directions, different viewpoints, and changing landscapes – perhaps the scenery which Barry felt was the most appropriate, both for himself and for the rest of us.

References

Armstrong, D. (1995) *Power and Partnership in Education*, London, Routledge

Ball, S. (1997) Policy sociology and critical social research: a personal review of recent education policy and policy research, *British Educational Research Journal*, special edition 1997, Reflexive Accounts of Education Reform

Duncker, P. (1996) *Hallucinating Foucault*, London, Serpents' Tail

Foster, P., Gomm, R., and Hammersley, M. (1996) *Constructing Educational Inequality*, London, Falmer

Fraser, N. (1992) The uses and abuses of French discourse theories, in N. Fraser and S. Bartsky (Eds.) *Revaluing French Feminism: Critical Essays on Difference, Agency, and Culture*, Indianapolis, Indiana University

Griffiths, M. and Troyna, B. (1995) Introduction, in M. Griffiths and B. Troyna (eds.) *Antiracism, Culture and Social Justice in Education*, Stoke, Trentham

Hatcher, R. and Troyna, B. (1994) The policy cycle: a Ball by Ball account, *Journal of Education Policy* 9, 2, pp. 155-170

Oliver, D. (1991) 'Active Citizenship in the 1990s', *Parliamentary Affairs* 140, pp.157-171

Skeggs, B. (1991) Review essay: Postmodernism: what is the fuss all about?, *British Journal of Sociology of Education*, 12, (2), pp.255-267

Troyna, B. (1993) *Racism and Education*, Buckingham, Open University Press

Troyna, B. (1994) 'Blind Faith? Empowerment and Educational Research' *International Studies in Sociology of Education*, 4, 1, pp. 3-24

Troyna, B. (1994a) Critical social research and education policy, *British Journal of Educational Studies*, 42, 1, pp.70-84

Troyna, B. (1994b) Reforms, research and being reflexive about being reflective, in D. Halpin and B. Troyna (Eds.) *Researching education policy: ethical and methodological issues,* London, Falmer

Troyna B., and Carrington B., (1990) *Education, Racism and Reform,* London, Routledge

Troyna, B. and Vincent, C. (1995) The discourses of social justice in education, *Discourse,* 16, 2, pp.149-166

Troyna, B. and Vincent, C. (1996) 'The ideology of expertism': the framing of special education and racial equality policies in the local state, in C. Christensen and F. Rizvi (Eds.) *Disability and the dilemmas of education and justice,* Buckingham, Open University Press

Troyna, B. and Williams, J., (1986) *Racism, Education and the State,* London, Croom Helm

Wellman, B., Carrington, P. and Hall, A. (1988) Networks as personal communities, in B. Wellman and S. Berkowitz (Eds.) *Social Structures: A Network Approach,* Cambridge, Cambridge University Press

2

BARRY TROYNA AS ENLIGHTENED RATIONALIST

SALLY TOMLINSON

In the mid-1990s Warwick University lost two Professors – both in their early 40s – to cancer. Professor of Philosophy Gillian Rose, died in December 1995, Professor of Education Barry Troyna, died in February 1996. Both died childless, but both achieved the other kind of immortality, a legacy of ideas, written down in books and papers to be discussed and debated, stimulating and challenging others to consider and reconsider their ideas. This is a legacy of permanent dialogue.

In this paper I want to consider Barry's contribution to partisan antiracist research and secondly, the contribution he made to an understanding of the salience of race in the way young people come to understand the world they live in. I find a link between the work of the two Professors: in Gillian's work on eighteenth century enlightenment rationalism, and in Barry's passionate commitment to the belief that, through an understanding of the processes that create and recreate racial discrimination and racial hatreds, racialised structures and discourses, racist postures and practices, action could be taken to change the society. Enlightenment rationalists of the eighteenth century believed that prejudice, superstition, conservative traditionalism and illegitimate authority, could be substituted by disinterested truth, objective judgements, and, literally, enlightenment, provided that people had the resolution and courage to use and apply critical intelligence (Rose, 1995).

Barry applied his critical intelligence to researching areas as diverse as race and the media, minority youth in the labour market, extremist organisations, teachers and race, children's understandings of race, local education authority policies, the effects of the 1988 Education Act on equal opportunities, and educational strategies for creating racial equality. His detailed ethnographic work, as Fazal Rizvi (1993, p. 15) has pointed out, cannot be divorced from an advocacy role and a clear commitment to social justice and racial equality. Those with such a commitment are the inheritors of enlightenment rationalism, optimistically believing that their work will have an impact and that the application of critical intelligence will help produce a better society.

Despite bouts of pessimism, Barry's commitment remained intact. As he put it himself:

> I would not like my involvement in the maelstrom of race and education to be seen as a disinterested chronicler of trends and patterns. In the 1950s and 1960s Tottenham, in North London, was a major area for the settlement of Afro-Caribbeans. I grew up with and went to school with black youth, and witnessed the racial abuse they experienced within and beyond the school gates. As the son of Jewish parents, I witnessed and experienced similar forms of harassment, especially from the racist and anti-Semitic activities of the British Movement and the National Front – the burning of synagogues, racist graffiti, physical and verbal abuse. So I am not embarrassed by my long standing involvement in this debate. On the contrary, it is a commitment that I wish to continue. (Troyna, 1993, p. vii)

This commitment was articulated through avowed partisan antiracist research, and the encouragement of others who took a similar partisan stance. He wrote eloquently of his early disillusionment with the policies and practices of multicultural education, his espousal of nascent antiracist approaches, his growing under-standing of the tenacity of deracialised policy approaches in educa-tion, and in the 1990s defended his partisan position vigorously, most notably in exchanges via academic articles with Martyn

Hammersley, Roger Gomm, Peter Foster, David Gillborn and David Drew (see Troyna, 1995; Foster, Gomm, Hammersley, 1996). I was sent much of this exchange for refereeing, by journal editors anxious for reassurance that the debate was academically respectable.

My own position, argued over with Barry for sixteen years, is as far as multiculturalism is concerned, closer to that outlined by Rex in this volume than to Barry's in that I have never felt antiracism could be divorced from multiculturalism and as far as partisan research is concerned, closer to the Weberian tradition espoused by Foster *et al.* But the debate over partisan research, particularly in the area of race and education, is important and should continue. Barry's account of 'doing partisan research' as it articulates with antiracist principles, outlined in Troyna (1995), is an honest advocacy of the view that a researcher's political commitments and declared values should shape and direct the research, and he may be correct to assert that 'all research, from its conception ... reflects a partisanship which derives from the social identity and values of the researcher' (p. 403). In race research this was an issue opened up for discussion by Gunnar Mrydal in his methodological appendix to 'An American Dilemma' (1944). Mrydal's view, as Barry himself noted, was that it is only when value premises are stated explicitly that it is possible to determine how valid the research conclusions are.

Partisan commitment however, can lead to over-enthusiastic condemnation of those who are working for the creation of a more equitable society from less overt value positions. It was mistaken, as Barry almost conceded to me in one discussion, to attack the Swann Report, *Education for All* (DES, 1985), so vigorously, accusing the committee of eschewing responsibility for reformulating the education system to deal with an ethnically diverse clientele, and bracketing the liberal Lords Swann and Scarman, with the right-wing commentators Honeyford, Flew and Scruton (Troyna, 1987, p 8). In fact, the political interventions of Swann and Scarman, both in their reports and through their parliamentary activities, were important in curbing more extreme opposition to multiculturalism and antiracism, during the 1980s.

Partisan research also risks so close an association with political movements that it neglects to analyse the values, ideologies and commitments of the opposition. Barry noted that Lee Harvey had advocated a critical social research that included 'overt political struggle against oppressive social structures' (Harvey, 1990, p 2) and that an increasing number of antiracists, feminists, and neo-Marxist theorists had adopted this position. For them, unmasking oppressive structures and contributing to social and political change can come to be the *raison d'être* for research. However, what actually happened in the UK in the 1980s, was that while antiracists sought to define their research and activities as separate from those labelled multiculturalists, and engaged in conceptual debates over definitions of multiculturalism and antiracism, only a limited amount of actual race research, from a critical or any other perspective, was actually carried out. Meanwhile, the white majority population continued to be much more influenced by those who sought to deny the reality and permanence of a multiracial British society, and to deny the claims of minority citizens to be included within the boundaries of the national identity.

Ultimately though, Barry's major commitment to partisan research, was to advocate reflexivity, explicit value premise, triangulation of data and ethical approaches, rather than link research to overt political action. His courage in creating a debate which will continue is one of his legacies.

By the mid-1980s Barry had begun to research the questions which he considered to be at the heart of debates on race and education. How is the concept of race conceptualised and internalised? Why and under what circumstances is race such an appealing way of constructing the world and creating a distinct mode of reasoning even in very young children? How is it that racism comes to achieve such an important position in the way many white children make sense of their lives? These questions became particularly important when he moved to work for two years in what was then Sunderland Polytechnic in the North-East of England. It was there that he began to engage with 'teaching race' in white contexts, and, with Libby

Selman, began an action-research project on implementing multicultural and antiracist education in mainly white colleges. The project started from the understanding that antiracist intervention would go nowhere if young white people were merely blamed for their racist beliefs and practices, 'preaching at skin-heads' as John Rex once described it. The aims of the research were to help all students recognise that they shared various forms of inequality – as students, as women, as working-class people – with racial minorities, but also to help them to analyse the specific nature of racial inequality and racist discourse.

One outcome of this research was the production of an outline, 'Framework for multicultural and antiracist education', which was intended for use, and is used, by teachers in schools and colleges (see Troyna and Selman, 1991, p.7 reprinted in Troyna, 1993, p.134). This kind of material assistance for practitioners, along with the advocacy model on which it is based, is enlightenment rationalism in action!

On his return to Warwick University in 1988 as Lecturer, then Reader, later Professor, Barry was concerned to develop a deeper understanding of the salience of race in the lives of young children and the way racial attitudes, in social-psychological terminology, are created and re-created in each generation of young people. In 1989 he began work with Richard Hatcher on young white children's perceptions and interpretations of their everyday social worlds, which whether or not they had encountered racial minorities, included racial frameworks of interpretation (Troyna and Hatcher, 1992). This work recognised that after over fifty years of research in the USA and elsewhere on racial attitudes and racial identities, Laskar's 1929 conclusion that 'children are made to notice differences and accept them as signs of inner difference of value' (Laskar, 1929, p. 370) still held. Research in Britain has certainly demonstrated that young children use racial frames of reference by the time they begin primary school, although there has been a history of reluctance among teachers to recognise that there is no age of 'racial innocence'.

The Troyna-Hatcher study took further, understandings of the dynamic way in which racial beliefs and racist ideologies are used by children. Race and racism are significant features of the cultures of white and mainly-white primary schools. But racism has a conditional status – it is conditional on the extent to which it helps children to make sense of their own lives and resolve their own conflicts. Children actively select and interpret messages about race, and are capable of holding inconsistent and contradictory attitudes. However, while racism is strong in the lives of white children, 'antiracist attitudes and behaviour, and the presence of racially egalitarian elements in the thinking even of children who engage in racist behaviour, are a crucial factors on which teachers can build' (Troyna and Hatcher, 1992, p. 207). It must be said that neither teachers nor children are helped by the absence in the curriculum of anything approximating to political education, which might put race in the context of the economic and social structures of the society.

While the Troyna-Hatcher research was in progress, I had been researching the fate of formal attempts to bring multicultural and antiracist education into white schools. My study also indicated that pupils in white areas held contradictory views of minorities, with an emphasis on negative evaluation, displaying antagonism, hostility and xenophobia, but also found evidence of a recognition among white pupils of the unfairness of racial discrimination and a fraternalist desire for more knowledge of minorities. 'Rather than simply describing the young people's beliefs as racist, and expressing moral condemnation ... there is a need to distinguish the various beliefs expressed and examine possible reasons for their strengths and persistence' (Tomlinson, 1990, p. 45).

I discussed with Barry the importance of an historical perspective, which I felt was lacking in his work. He took for granted that ideologies of race and racism were a product of colonial-imperialism, and that the curriculum and teachers' views reflected this. I felt that there had been insufficient work linking ethnocentric beliefs in Empire, white superiority and militaristic patriotism. Until relatively recently these were uncritically reflected in textbooks, and were further reinforced by pedagogic techniques which encouraged simplification of complex moral issues and an acceptance of value-laden curriculum content. Neither has the resistance to the creation of a national curriculum fit for a multicultural, multiracial society, been the subject of much research; yet the salience and persistence of white racist beliefs is still in the late 1990s, reinforced via the curriculum, in schools, colleges and also in higher education.

Barry's concern to probe the meaning and salience of race would, I think, have led to an appreciation of a new focus in the study of race and racism. This is the appearance of 'white studies' – a recent body of literature on the history and experience of being white (see Bonnett, 1996). Barry would have appreciated the 1997 Reith lectures, given by Patricia Williams, a black Professor of Law at Columbia University, New York, who noted in her second lecture that 'Perhaps one reason why conversations about race are so often doomed to frustration is that the notion of whiteness as race is almost never implicated' (Williams, 1997). As she explained, one of the more difficult legacies of slavery and colonialism is the degree to which racism's tenacious hold is manifest not just through class, education or neighbourhood, but through the non-examination of whiteness as a racial identity. Whiteness is assumed to be beyond the realms of race, white children who see and mark others as black, never learn to see or know themselves as white. They are the normal, the unraced, those spared the 'affliction' of race.

Barry had long moved from any view of white as agent, black as victim or resister, but he would be intrigued by the possibilities opened up by the examination of whiteness as race and the contribution his own work had made to reaching out towards this possibility.

I have characterised Barry as an inheritor of the tradition of enlightenment rationalism. The 18th century enlightenment philosophers *were* optimistic in their belief that knowledge about the world could only lead to social improvement. The events of the 19th and 20th centuries have severely tested optimism about the way the human species treats its fellow members, particularly as far as the exploitation and dehumanisation of racially-designated groups is concerned. Researchers in the race area can avoid critical theorising, difficult research, and the necessity of value commitment, in attempting to interpret and change the world. This was not Barry's way. He embraced commitment, recognised the dialectic of knowledge and action and retained a justifiable optimistic belief that his work would have some positive effect.

References

Bonnett, A. (1996) 'White Studies', The problems and projects of a New Research Agenda', *Theory, Culture and Society,* Vol. 13, No. 2, pp 145-155

DES (1985) *Education for All* (The Swann Report), London, HMSO

Foster, P., Gomm, R., Hammersley, M. (1996) *Constructing Educational Inequality,* Lewes, Falmer

Harvey, L. (1990) *Critical Social Research,* London, Allen and Unwin

Laskar, B. (1929) *Race Attitudes in Young Children,* New York, Greenwood Press

Myrdal, G. (1944) *An American Dilemma,* New York, Harper

Rizvi, F. (1993) 'Critical Introduction – Researching racism and education' in Troyna, B., *Racism and Education,* Buckingham, Open University Press

Rose, G. (1995) *Love's Work* London, Vintage

Tomlinson, S. (1990) *Multicultural Education in White Schools,* London, Batsford

Troyna, B. (ed.) (1987) *Racial Inequality in Education,* London, Tavistock

Troyna, B. (1993) *Racism in Education,* Buckingham, Open University Press

Troyna, B. (1995) 'Beyond Reasonable Doubt? Researching Race in Educational Settings', *Oxford Review of Education,* Vol. 21, No. 4, pp 393-408

Troyna, B. and Hatcher, R. (1992) *Racism in Children's Lives,* London, Routledge

Troyna, B. and Selman, L. (1991) *Implementing Multicultural and Antiracist Education in Mainly White Colleges,* London, Further Education Unit at the DfE

Williams, P. (1997) 'The Genealogy of Race: Towards a Theory of Grace', *The 2nd Reith Lecture BBC Radio 4,* 1/3/97

3

BARRY TROYNA AS CRITICAL SOCIAL RESEARCHER

DAVID HALPIN

In her moving testimony to the high quality of Barry Troyna's teaching and the support he offered as a PhD supervisor, which was published last year in the *Journal of Education Policy*, Carol Vincent states 'there was no sense that his work existed outside of himself, [as] a series of abstract tasks that could be objectively, neutrally, dealt with' (1996, p.287). Writing of himself, just over four years ago, Barry went further, declaring that he was 'committed to the integration of antiracist and related egalitarian convictions into the design, execution and interpretation' of his research (Troyna, 1993a, p.168).

This position, of course, has a much longer history. For throughout his distinguished and sadly foreshortened career as a university academic, Barry was concerned always to articulate his work as a researcher with his political activism – indeed, he considered each to be the obverse of the other. As a self-styled 'critical social scientist', Barry was concerned to undertake research as the basis for the development of strategies of social transformation (see Troyna, 1994a, for more about this). In this connection, he was fond of quoting from Lee Harvey's book, *Critical Social Research* (1990), in particular the following passages with which he closely identified:

'Critical social research does not take the apparent social structure, social processes, or accepted history for granted. It tries to dig beneath the surface of appearances. It asks how social systems really work, how ideology or history conceals the processes which oppress and control people ... [But] not only does it want to show what is happening, it is also concerned with doing something about it. Critical social research includes an overt political struggle against oppressive structures' (Harvey, 1990, pp.6 and 20).

The resonance here with Marx's famous aphorism is clear enough. How does it go?: 'The philosophers have only interpreted the world in various ways, the point is to change it' (*Thesis on Feuerbach*, 1845).

Barry's political-academic project, and others like it, is also illuminated by another of Marx's insights, this time about the labour process: 'Man not only effects a change of form in the materials of nature; he also realises his own purposes in those materials' (*Capital*, Volume 1, 1867). In Barry's case, doing social research was always about 'making a statement' – simultaneously about himself and about an aspect of the social world that troubled him and for which he sought the means of making a change for the better. And the political changes to which he dedicated his life's work as a university teacher and researcher were, as if we need to be reminded, to do with social justice, 'race', and the educational process. In 'realising his own purposes' in this way Barry was incapable of distinguishing between his political and professional values, and simply couldn't understand why others tried to – in fact he found this unintelligible – nor why they felt he should try as well. It is this incredulity on his part that informs the debate which he entered into towards the end of his life with Peter Foster, Roger Gomm and Martyn Hammersley (see Troyna, 1995), about which I will say a little more later.

Barry's political commitment left, in his words, 'an indelible mark' on the way he approached research. To that extent, he was always explicit about the sort of 'bias' he was seeking to mobilise. Indeed, because he wore his ideological commitments on his sleeve, there was never any confusion about where he was coming from. That did not mean that he was incapable of walking up, as he came to see them, one or two blind-alleys. In the autobiographical preface to his book, *Racism and Education* (1993b), for example, he writes very self-critically of his previous, but subsequently abandoned, naive belief in the empowering potential of multicultural education. A similar tendency is manifest in the introductory chapter of a book he and I edited together in 1994 in which he comments sceptically on specific contributions to that genre of writings in educational research which gives prominence to 'being reflexive' (Troyna, 1994b), concluding – much to my anguish at the time – with a remark that queried the very rationale of our joint enterprise!

Barry's ideological transparency and his willingness to subject his own ideas and those of others to critical reflection were, then, recurring features of his work. There was a sort of drivenness about his approach to academic life as well which is reflected in his prolific output and productivity generally. He worked very hard, very hard indeed, to put on record regularly his version of the truth, both about the reality of racism in schools and, in more recent times, the manner in which he went about constructing that reality. Paradoxically, his drivenness made him a kind of 'methodological purist' (Troyna, 1995) – a term of gentle abuse he actually invented to describe the work of some of his critics. What I mean here is that, while Barry eschewed a foundationalist view of the nature of the research process and rejected all claims to objectivity and neutrality, he had a highly principled and profoundly moral point of view about what he was doing as a researcher, an attitude of mind and of practice, in fact, that may sometimes have made him insufficiently sensitive to legitimate concerns about his research. Indeed, Martyn Hammersley detects in Barry a paradoxical tendency to require of his critics that they justify their points of view about his work with 'more evidence than would be judged necessary by any reasonable person' (Hammersley, 1993, p.339). Significantly, though, this did not prevent Barry from regarding Martyn's own work very highly. I suspect this admiration derived from a recognition that Martyn, like himself, was anxious to pursue, *to the limit*, debate and discussion about the constitutive principles of social research.

Barry's convictions as researcher-political activist contributed ultimately to a decision on his part to write a book about education research methodology, in particular about the nature and legitimacy of 'partisan research'. Sadly, his premature death means that this will never be realised. However, among his existing publications and conference contributions there are more than a few hints available as to the sort of book he might have written. In this regard, it is important to record that Barry's fascination with the methodological character of antiracist research predates considerably his more recent exchanges with Martyn Hammersley and Roger Gomm. In 1989, for instance, he published, with Bruce Carrington, a chapter in an edited collection entitled 'Whose side are we on? Ethical dilemmas in research on race and education' in which he defended the view that antiracist educational ideology is congruent with research informed by critical theory. There were other contributions in this vein in the years that followed (see Troyna, 1991, for example), culminating in 1994 in a typically strident discussion of the nature and relevance of 'critical social research' in a special edition of the *British Journal of Educational Studies* devoted to education policy studies.

The previous year, Barry contributed a provocative paper to the Fifth International Conference on Educational Evaluation held at Hughes Hall, Cambridge. The conference was concerned 'to develop a critical review of evaluation policy and practice over the last twenty years and to begin to elaborate new theoretical and methodological strategies for the future' (Stronach and Torrance, 1995, p.283). Barry had been invited to the conference to offer a 'discrepant voice'. He obliged his audience by outlining a view of educational research tied to political commitment rather than disinterested enquiry:

> The voice of antiracist ... research (*he declared*) is distinctive only insofar as its vocalists are in the same choir (*Barry's penchant for metaphors and analogies was well to the fore on this occasion*). They do not, however, all sing the same song; nor are they necessarily in the same key. Their voices and choice of

repertoire may well sound discordant to the ears of policy makers and certain colleagues in the 'academy' (*for which read 'methodological purists'*). This is related to their predilection towards qualitative research traditions; a tendency to adopt a standpoint epistemology; and a commitment to ensuring that social justice issues remain on the research and policy agenda despite the pervasive equiphobic climate' (Stronach and Torrance, 1995, p.285).

By 'standpoint epistemology', Barry meant to refer to the fact that he was concerned to 'foreground' racialised relations, distancing himself, as I have already remarked, from notions of neutrality or value freedom and the myths of objectivity. On the other hand – and this cannot be stressed enough – his political commitment did not lead him to engage in methodologically unprincipled research. On the contrary, as in aspects of his personal life, he subscribed to many of the *conventional* imperatives of the sociological project: to obtain data responsibly; to interrogate them rigorously; and to support arguments with evidence. Thus, it is, I think, a terrible misrepresentation on the joint parts of Peter Foster, Roger Gomm and Martyn Hammersley (1996) to suggest that Barry's approach 'represents an abandonment of research in favour of propaganda' (p.178). For it is one thing to subject to critical scrutiny the manner in which data have been used to support conclusions, (as Foster, Gomm and Hammersley do in the case, not just of Barry, but of Stephen Ball, David Gillborn, Sheila Riddell and Cecile Wright as well), quite another to argue that his work and theirs do not qualify as 'academic research' (see Foster, *et al*, 1996, p.32). In any event, it is simply not reasonable totally to judge and query the merits of research conducted within one methodological paradigm by the criteria of acceptability of another. No doubt Barry's critics would want to contest the legitimacy of my understanding of their critique of his work. In fact Martyn Hammersley (1993) is on record as saying that Barry himself seemed 'to regard the interrogation of his work by academic peers (such as Roger Gomm) as something that required explanation' (p.340). That's as maybe. All I can say is that that is not the Barry Troyna I knew, nor the one he himself wrote about in his own accounts of his own research. Such a charge moreover runs counter to the critical social scientific frame of reference within which he always conducted his enquiries.

It is, then, such a pity that we do not have Barry with us anymore to engage further with this important debate. His proposed book on methodology would have been a good read – typically provocative, inevitably sceptical, absolutely engaging and ultimately challenging. Certainly, it would have received – as do all the best books – very mixed and many reviews. And, to be sure, it would have found its way on to the reading lists of most courses in research methods in education, no doubt sitting uncomfortably, but interestingly, alongside that of Foster, Gomm and Hammersley (1996).

References

Foster, P., Gomm. R. and Hammersley, M. (1996) *Constructing Educational Inequality: An Assessment of Research on School Processes*, London, Falmer

Harvey, L. (1990) *Critical Social Research*, London, Allen and Unwin

Hammersley, M. (1993) On methodological purism: a response to Barry Troyna, *British Educational Research Journal*, 19 (4), 339-341

Stronach, I. and Torrance, H. (1995) The future of evaluation: a retrospective, *Cambridge Journal of Education*, 25 (3), 283-299

Troyna, B. (1991) Children, 'race' and racism: the limitations of research and policy, *British Journal of Educational Studies*, 39 (4), 425-436

Troyna, B. (1993a) Underachiever or misunderstood? A reply to Roger Gomm, *British Educational Research Journal*, 19 (2), 167-174

Troyna, B. (1993b) *Racism and Education*, Buckingham, Open University Press

Troyna, B. (1994a) Critical social research and education policy, *British Journal of Educational Studies*, 42 (1), 70-84

Troyna, B. (1994b) Reforms, research and being reflexive about being reflective, In Halpin, D. and Troyna, B. (Eds.) *Researching Education Policy: Ethical and Methodological Issues,* London, Falmer

Troyna, B. (1995) Beyond reasonable doubt? Researching 'race' in educational settings, *Oxford Review of Education*, 21 (4), 395-408

Troyna, B. and Carrington, B. (1989) Whose side are we on? Ethical dilemmas in research on 'race' and education, In Burgess, R.G. (Ed.) *The Ethics of Educational Research*, Lewes, Falmer

Vincent, C. (1996) Tribute to Professor Barry Troyna, *Journal of Education Policy*, 11 (3), 287-288

4

BARRY AND THE BRITISH EDUCATIONAL RESEARCH ASSOCIATION

Jean Rudduck

> Bolshieness I have always admired – its potential as a purposeful kickback by the powerless against the powerful, in society and in education. (*BERA-Research Intelligence*, 1997, p.25).

So wrote Dave Hill in a recent journal article. Dave's bolshiness, in the good radical creative tradition, sought to enliven the teacher education scene – a scene where compliance is the foundation of institutional survival, rather than one which welcomes 'purposeful kickbacks'. As he acknowledged, given the 'the effective removal of almost anything 'critical' and 'oppositional' from teacher education courses', his views stood out strongly but also too starkly and he consequently found himself without a job.

By comparison, Barry's bolshieness found expression in two very different contexts where radical thinking was less of a liability. One was race, the other was research. It is research that I want to concentrate on.

Barry knew that you were more likely to have an impact if you spoke from the in-, rather than the out-side. His dilemma was how to get inside without compromising his values or, put another way, how to be radical without becoming radical chic. With consummate strategical skill, he managed to avoid the trap by moving inside in two ways. First, he situated himself, within the British Educational Research Association (BERA), in a position where he could pursue his values without impediment – providing that he could win the support of his committee, which it seems that he did, easily. He took on the responsibility of editor of the *British Educational Research Journal* (BERJ) and became a co-opted member of the BERA Council, where he was able to address his concerns about risk and renewal in research. We (members of the BERA Council, and members of BERA more generally) knew that Barry would 'use' his position in the way that good newspaper editors do, to pursue the values that he believed in while maintaining an unfaultable commitment to quality and sufficient links with the past for his change of policy to be seen to evolve rather than to erupt.

Second, he stood for quality and the excellence of his own track record in research on ethnicity was widely recognised. He combined the tough leg work of a field researcher with the inclinations of a theorist. As John Eggleston said at the BERA memorial seminar, he was a man on the edge of being one of the greats of his time (and as Christopher Fry said, 'A coming man, already gone'), memorable for his cool but passionate, bold yet unswerving, commitment to the pursuit of social justice. He had a professional base, rooted in his reputation as a researcher, which gave him credibility and respect, and he had an institutional base – within BERA – which gave him additional openings for his ideas. He used these bases to pursue the goals of quality in research and the cause of the 'new researcher'.

Thus: he was a member of the BERA Working Party on Quality, convened by Wynne Harlen, and contributed to a symposium on quality issues at the annual conference in 1994: but it was his editorship of BERJ that particularly gave him scope to follow and debate his concern with questions of quality. Ann Lewis, who worked with him on BERJ, comments:

> Barry was passionate about BERJ, proud to be Editor and strongly committed to doing all he could to ensure that BERJ met the highest possible academic standards. His vision for the Journal was not rooted in conventional wisdoms but in a search for excellence. He had many plans to extend and enrich the style and foci of BERJ. These plans were based on a demand for rigour and merit, not novelty. He enjoyed the debates that took place in editorial meetings and loved the fierce arguments over

topics like anonymous refereeing or positive discrimination in submissions. (Letter, 1997; quoted with permission)

With regard to his commitment to new researchers, I remember him at a BERA conference, some years ago, asking, from an outsider perspective, who got funded by the ESRC and whether good but relatively unknown researchers could apply for grants with any optimism or whether grants tended to go, especially when money was tight, to researchers with a recognised reputation. His questions, asked unflinchingly, cut right through to the heart of a set of crucial issues in research – issues of risk and renewal. It was not surprising, therefore, that as a member of the BERA Council he chose to make support for new researchers a major focus of activity. This focus also reflected his concern to support those who have difficulty in making their voices heard.

The agenda that Barry pursued, with the help of other members of Council, Rosemary Deem in particular, took shape and at the annual conference at Oxford in September, 1994 (BERA's 25th anniversary), Donald McIntyre and his team of organisers launched a special event for new researchers which has since become a regular feature of annual conferences, with the new researchers themselves taking responsibility for determining the agenda for their sessions. They also participate more widely in other conference sessions.

At the same time, an idea that Barry and Colin Harrison had articulated took shape. The purpose was, again, to underline the importance of the work of our new researchers. A structure was set up by the BERA Council, with appropriate regulations drafted initially by Barry, to recognise and reward the outstanding student dissertation of those successfully completed during the last year. The winner's expenses were paid to attend the BERA conference in order to receive the award and there was also a small cheque. The event was in part a symbolic act, reminding established researchers of their responsibility to support those at the starting gate in times where advancement and security are much more elusive than they were when a lot of us started our careers. The first award was also made at the Oxford conference in 1994.

This was the right time to make new researchers a priority. It chimed with ESRC policy on training in reflecting a national concern about new blood in the research community and long term career prospects. There was anxiety lest the Higher Education Funding Council's research assessment exercises were, unwittingly, leading to the marginalisation of research students. The logical outcome of the 'transfer market' (where departments sought to sign up, before the audit date of the next exercise, researchers with a string of prestigious publications and a dowry of externally funded research projects) was to increase the amount of money invested in senior staff – with the consequence that new researchers were likely to find fewer openings and resources to support them. BERA, through Barry and others, was concerned to keep high on the agenda the need to ensure a flow of high quality people who can take their place in the research community with commitment and confidence.

Another side effect of the research selectivity exercise was that the established and prestigious journals were all hanging up 'No Vacancies' signs and tending to be 'full' several editions ahead. New researchers were finding it difficult to get published and to build up a respectable *CV*, unless they wrote in tandem with experienced researchers, or submitted to journals with special policies to disseminate the work of new comers. Barry's concern about this development went beyond his work on the BERA Council and BERJ. For instance, one of his last publications was a book edited with Morwenna Griffiths, *Antiracism, Culture and Social Justice in Education*, launched at the 1995 BERA conference. In the words of the editors the book 'provides a platform for a number of new voices' from 'a variety of educational settings'. Many of the contributors had given papers at a symposium, Race and Culture, co-ordinated by Barry and Morwenna in 1994. Their intention had been to give visibility to 'new perspectives' and 'emerging material'. Indeed, an explicit criterion for invitation to contribute to both symposium and book was to be a 'researcher.. relatively new on the scene'.

The voices in the book resonate strongly with the voices being heard in the American Educational Research Association (AERA). William Russell, reviewing the role and emerging policy of AERA, argues that 'Ethnic and gender research and scholarship must be viewed as a valuable intellectual pursuit within AERA and academe not only for its substantive, cutting-edge contributions but also as a vehicle to attract students of colour to the community'. He comments on the 'tragically small' numbers of minority groups entering research and post secondary teaching as a career, and he goes on to note that:

> The increased demand for knowledge and understanding about minorities and education ... demands a strong cadre of minority researchers who can and must contribute creative, non-traditional perspectives on what should be done in classrooms, schools, and curriculum inasmuch as traditional approaches have not sufficed. (1994, pp.27-28)

As editor of BERJ, Barry had another avenue for supporting new researchers and Ann Lewis comments:

> He was often kind and supportive of new writers and researchers. He would encourage such people with lengthy, informal advice about submissions and had a gentle turn of phrase when writing to them. One of my favourites was 'Your statistics are rather too sophisticated for many of our readers'. His impatience was reserved for those long-standing academics whom he felt to be riding off younger researchers or out-dated reputations. (From a letter, 1997; quoted with permission.)

The issues that Barry raised within BERA were part of an international zeitgeist about the health, and wealth, of educational research. Seamus Hegarty's lecture to mark the 25th anniversary of the National Foundation for Educational Research leads with the statement, 'Educational research is – once again – going through a period of reflection and challenge and, hopefully, renewal' and the issue of how and where we 'prepare people for a research career' is a key theme. In their review, 'Educational Research and Development in OECD Countries', McGaw, Kogan and Tuijnman take up the issue of 'new researchers':

> There is an urgent need in many countries to review the career paths of educational R and D personnel to ensure that the returns on societal and individual investment in training are maximised. (1996, p7)

James Calderhead, in the first presidential address of the European Educational Research Association, explored a similar set of issues and pointed to the 'generally low level of training of educational researchers' compared with training in other academic fields of enquiry (1996, p5).

Barry's persistent challenge to us to 'see' how resolutely the habits of power relations hold inequity in place is relevant beyond his substantive area of Research, racism; it holds also for the structuring of the research community. If we are to keep faith with his hopes for the future we must continue to find ways of examining the social structures and institutional infrastructures that make access and recognition difficult and we must continue to develop strategies for achieving a more widespread and authentic respect for new researchers and what they can contribute to the process of renewal in research and in research communities.

References

Calderhead, J. (1996) Europeanisation of educational research, *EERA Bulletin*, 2,3,308, December

Eggleston, J. (1996) Obituary: Professor Barry Troyna, *British Journal of Sociology of Education*, 17,4,507-508

Griffiths, M. and Troyna, B. (1995) *Antiracism, Culture and Social Justice in Education*, Stoke on Trent, Trentham

Hegarty, S. (1996) Educational Research in Context, opening address of the conference to mark the 25th anniversary of the NFER, December 1996

Hill, D. (1997) Critical research and the dismissal of dissent, *Research Intelligence*, no.59, 25-26, February

McGaw, B., Kogan, M. and Tuijnman, A. (1996) Educational research in OECD Countries, *EERA Bulletin*, 2,1,3-12, March

Russell, W.J. (1994) 'Achieving Diversity in Academe', *Educational Researcher* 23, 9, pp.26-28

5

THE OTHER SIDE OF WRITING: PUBLISHING AND SOCIAL JUSTICE[1]

Gaby Weiner

Roland Barthe referred to biography as 'a novel that dare not speak its name'. In preparing this short essay, I have become aware that it can also be an autobiography that dare not speak its name. In thinking about someone else's life, it is inevitable to recall one's own, to explore the coincidences and similarities, the discontinuities and disagreements between biographer and biographee. I have thus found myself centrally implicated in the story I wanted to tell about Barry Troyna, finding some difficulty also in constructing a coherent story because my memories of him seem so fragmentary and elusive. Yet, if the reader is to draw any meaning at all, biography needs to take a recognisable narrative form, and this is what I have struggled to achieve. Biography also necessarily involves some form of selection and shaping, which was made easier for me by the fact that I was asked to concentrate on a particular and perhaps minor aspect of Barry's work: his term of editorship, following mine, of the *British Educational Research Journal* (BERJ) and on our joint research project exploring the politics and practices of academic journal publishing[2]. In fulfilling my commission I offer suggestions for what made him want to be involved, in an editorial capacity, in the production of academic knowledge because, I think, we shared similar views.

We also shared similar backgrounds. We were both brought up in Jewish households in North London. I was as fanatical a supporter of Arsenal as Barry was of Spurs, until I discovered that the Football Association rules asserted that girls and women were ineligible to play alongside boys and men – something to do with inadequate changing rooms, I believe! I lost interest after that, although Barry clearly never did – a gender divide that was never resolved. We took from our own particular ethnic backgrounds a wish to fight against persecution and discrimination: for him it was against racism, for me it was this, but other things too, especially sexism and sex discrimination. For both of us, the aim was to challenge and, to some extent, obliterate the unfairness and injustice that had done so much harm to Jewish people of our parents' generation.

My earliest memory of Barry was at a British Educational Research Association (BERA) regional conference organised by Stephen Ball and Tony Green in London in the early 1980s. Barry gave an impassioned paper on the importance of antiracist perspectives in education for which he was roundly attacked by some black women in the audience for his audacity, as a white man, in daring to take the floor on such issues. It needs to be remembered that metropolitan radicalism was at its strongest at this period, with people competing to occupy the loftiest of moral high grounds (myself included). Anyhow, Barry managed to complete his presentation relatively unscathed, and I am sure, used the experience to argue his position more strongly when confronting similar challenges later in his career.

Barry's political commitment to his work was clear in the topics he chose to write about, and in his productivity, his lucidity and his passion. I too had a commitment to writing derived from the early days of the women's movement where it was argued that, as feminists, we needed to be able to communicate feminist ideas to all women, not just academics.

Why were we both attracted to journal editing? One reason perhaps was that we viewed it as a means of joining the academic *main-stream*, particularly in our work with BERJ. Coming from back-grounds that were deemed by many in English society as exotic and different, and from disciplinary areas that were seen as not quite legitimate because they were too bound up with politics and passion to be properly, 'objectively' academic, editing BERJ seemed to offer us the possibility of coming in from the periphery. To sit on BERA Council, to have an impact on publishing policy, and to gain a purchase on the hidden processes of academic scholarship, were fascinating and to some extent, vicarious pleasures. We saw journals as implicated in the production of knowledge, and BERJ as one gatekeeper affecting our own sphere of knowledge production – that of educational research

Radway (1984) argues that editors, readers and writers comprise powerful interpretative communities that organise around their texts to determine shared systems of cultural meaning. Barry and I shared a rather romantic view of the power of print. Like Gramsci who believed that a socialist press could create a ruling-class consciousness in the working class (Downing, 1980), we hoped that taking over editorship of BERJ would offer possibilities of challenging the hegemonic authority of conventional academia. However, as Audre Lorde famously asked, can the master's tools be used to dismantle the master's house? (Lorde, 1984). Could we pursue an overtly political agenda in the passionless landscape of footnotes and formulae, of chi-squares and measures of significance? To what extent could the liberalism of academic freedom be harnessed to a new academic agenda?

In fact, linking scholarship to politics proved to be less innovative than we originally thought. The first academic journals were created by nineteenth-century German historical scholars who found articulation of political convictions consistent with scholarly standards. In contrast, Anglo-American academics have been more likely to define themselves as apolitical and objective, though, significantly, this has not prevented some scholars from being penalised for promoting 'unpopular views'. McDermott (1994) offers a number of examples from the United States where academics were punished for their political views; for example, in upholding the right to strike, refusing to testify before the House Un-American Activities Committee, supporting the recognition of Communist China. It is only relatively recently, following the civil rights and feminism movements of the 1960s and 1970s, that journals have sought to tread the thin line dividing politics and scholarship.

Nevertheless, the issues addressed by such journals, for example, relating to social inequality or rights or involving critiques of hegemonic epistemologies, are still treated as biased and thus, not proper scholarship, by many academics. It was not so long ago that I was accused of being a 'conviction' researcher and of allowing my politics to intrude into the process of neutral enquiry which, it was argued, should be the main goal of educational researchers (see Weiner, 1990, for a discussion of this in relation to educational evaluation and social justice).

Involvement with the decidedly mainstream BERJ was, therefore, highly attractive to Barry and me. After he had been appointed editor-elect, we spent quite a lot of time together – he usually organised our meetings in London so that they coincided with Spurs fixtures. We discussed the everyday ins and outs of running a journal. He, like me, hoped to exert more influence on the journal than he was ultimately able to: perhaps because BERJ is too eclectic for other than a heavy reliance on referees and or because editors are limited to a three-year period of office and or because the flow of papers is relatively unpredictable. Even so, it is noticeable that during Barry's editorship there was an increase in articles on broadly social justice issues, perhaps because some researchers felt that their research topics might be treated more sympathetically by him.

We also spent much time gossiping about the various people that we had to deal with in the course of our time with the journal and in our working lives, recognising that some of the problems we experienced were due to our own volatility and impatience at the slowness of change. We shared a strong commitment to the culture of academia, yet at times were also sharply oppositional to and critical of it: a post-modern position which, according to Patti Lather (1991, p. 38) offers 'ways to work within and yet challenge dominant discourses'. This led to the schizoid position shared by other critics of the academy, of frequently wanting to bite the hand that fed us; that is, in wishing to succeed in a system of which we were deeply suspicious and judgmental. Journal editing appeared to counter this by creating a new space in which to work with an alternative set of goals and outcomes (and a fresh and attractive set of 3Rs – recognition, respectability, reputation).

As overlapping editors our relationship was mainly harmonious, except in one respect – Barry failed to maintain the database of BERJ submitted articles which I had laboured so hard to set up during my term of office. Barry's modernist tendencies did not extend, it would seem, to computers. He preferred manual technologies, although the quality of his editorial work was as rigorous and impressive as his writing. In fact, he was a highly competent and well organised editor with a clear view of policy and detail. My last conversation with him, several weeks before his death, took place when he rang to check whether Carrie Paechter and I were on time with our special BERJ issue on post-modernism and poststructualism (Paechter and Weiner, 1996).

Significantly, Barry was able to confer respectability on me when we managed at his first and my second, attempt to get our ESRC grant. There is no doubt that having Barry's name and the Warwick logo on the proposal eased referees' doubts concerning viability and practicality. The project offered us the opportunity to explore power relationships within academic publishing, of which we had become so aware as BERJ editors.

We were both delighted when news came through that we had received the grant, particularly because it provided both of us with an opportunity to move into different disciplinary areas. We were planning the details of the project just before Barry became ill for the last time in the autumn of 1995 and it seems especially poignant that one of the few times that he was able to enjoy seeing his professorial status confirmed in print was in the advert for the project's research assistant! Even though he is not here to see things through, his enthusiasm for the enterprise and his involvement in planning and implementation will continue to shape and influence the project for its duration.

What is there left then, to say about Barry's life and his death? His death has left me with an enormous sadness despite the fact that I was not among his closest friends. This sadness is not only because he died so young but also because of his influence on my thinking during our work together on BERJ and on the publishing project. We connected, if that is the right word, around our perceptions of otherness in the academy, and in our wish to become both within and against. The Barry Troyna with whom I worked (and socialised) was charming, sharply witty, mostly hopeful, ceaselessly driven and ambitious, profoundly streetwise, and organised and reliable. It is for these qualities, as much as for his other scholarly work, that I will continue to remember and appreciate him.

Notes

1. Revised version of presentation given at the annual conference of BERA, September, 1996.

2. 'Getting Published: a study of writing, refereeing and editing practices' (ESRC no. R000236291) began in April 1996 and finishes in April, 1998. The research team is Angela Packwood (University of Warwick), Margaret Scanlon and Gaby Weiner (both at South Bank University).

References

Downing, J. (1980) *The Media Machine* London, Pluto Press

Lather, P. (1991) *Getting Smart: Feminist Research and Pedagogy With/in the Post-modern* New York, Routledge

Lorde, A. (1984) 'The Master's Tools Will Never Dismantle the Master's House' in *Sister Outsider* Freedom California, Crossing

McDermott, P. (1994) *Politics and Scholarship: Feminist Academic Journals and the Production of Knowledge* Urbana and Chicago, University of Illinois Press

Paechter, C. and Weiner, G. (1996) 'Editorial' *British Educational Research Association Journal: Special Issue: Post-modernism and Post-structuralism in Educational Research* 22, 3, 267-272

Radway, J. (1984) *Reading the Romance: Women, Patriarchy and Popular Literature* Chapel Hill, University of North Carolina Press

Weiner, G. (1990) 'Ethical Practice in an Unjust World: Educational Evaluation and Social Justice' *Gender and Education* 2, 2, 231-238

6

THEORY INTO PRACTICE: BARRY TROYNA, THE PRIMARY SCHOOL GOVERNOR AND COLLEAGUE

Sandra Shipton

It is often said by teachers that academics should leave the comfort of their offices and spend some time in classrooms and schools finding out what life is really like before expounding their educational theories and policies. It would not have been appropriate to say this to Barry Troyna because already he was out there.

Barry was a governor of Edgewick Community Primary School, the school where I am headteacher, for nine years. During this time he was active in the classroom, as a teacher and as a 'helper' and he also participated in a range of extra-curricula activities. This was a period which saw fundamental educational change. It was also a time in which the worth of antiracist work in primary schools was questioned and challenged. Barry saw, at first hand, what all these things meant to staff, pupils, parents and governors. He was in a position to witness theory and policy being put in to practice and he was also able to bring what he saw to bear on his own theorising.

In this paper I want to reflect on Barry's involvement in the life of my school and to consider how his experiences there informed his academic work. In doing this I also want to show something of Barry as a person, as someone whose ideals and beliefs manifested themselves in his day to day life, in his personal and professional relationships.

Early days... 1988 and all that

Barry's relationship with the school began in 1988, a significant time for everyone involved in education in England and Wales. 1988 was the year of the Education Reform Act (ERA) which set in motion substantial changes and posed considerable challenges. The National Curriculum was introduced, as were Standard Assessment Tests (for 7, 11, and 14 year olds) which would be used to construct school performance league tables. These reforms posed difficulties for many teachers and schools and particularly, it seemed, for us at Edgewick where our school policy stated categorically that 'children are not empty vessels waiting to be filled'. Clearly our line was at odds with what appeared to be a knowledge based and didactic National Curriculum. Furthermore there was no mention of ethnicity, 'race' or multicultural education within the ERA and these were areas central to our development as a school as well as being central to Barry's antiracist work. ERA also extended the roles and responsibilities of school governors, making them ultimately responsible for the curriculum, staffing and the financial management of schools. Increasingly budgets were delegated to individual schools (under a scheme known as Local Management of Schools – LMS) rather than being held centrally by each Local Education Authority. Never one to avoid a challenge Barry, whose teaching background was in the secondary sector and higher education, became a primary school governor.

At this time I had only recently become a headteacher and many of the other governors were also new to the job. Our learning curve had to be, and was, a steep one.

While, on the whole, the governing body was made up of people who were supportive of the school, as is so often the case, they had very little experience of educational issues and practices, or of being in managerial positions of any kind.The prospect of taking on responsibility for running the school was, therefore, quite daunting for them. It would have been very easy for Barry to dominate in this situation. He was, after all, an academic, someone who had written books, someone who knew what was going on in education in a general sense. Yet it was at this point that Barry's principles, derived from his work in the field of multiculturalism and antiracism, came to the fore. He could have been a figure that other members of the governing body were wary, if not downright scared of, but he managed to support his fellow governors in such a way as to give them confidence in their own abilities without being overbearing and without stifling them. His belief in the importance of relationships in any antiracist or equal opportunities work was put into practice, as was his ability to confront and destroy stereotypes. The governing body, which was made up of a cross section of white and Asian parents, political appointees and staff of the school, readily accepted Barry as a governor and as a friend. Within a year he was elected as Chair, a post which he reluctantly accepted and saw very much as being temporary. He aimed to step down as soon as possible and actively worked towards others taking on the responsibility by involving and supporting colleagues as much as he could.

Whilst he was enabling and supportive of the development of governors he was always willing to stand up and argue for pupils, parents and staff in matters of fairness and justice. He did this both with government departments, particularly regarding issues around the lack of an antiracist perspective in the content of the National Curriculum, and with the LEA. He soon became well known within the Education Department of the City Council. He definitely gave the school a high profile, whether he was fighting for improved Section 11 funding, changes in the LMS formula, or money for translation for governors' meetings. Officers of the LEA were sometimes perturbed to see him arrive at the regular meetings for Heads and Chairs of Governors, since such commitment was unusual. Never one to suffer fools gladly, he would challenge whenever he felt it was necessary, never backing off from difficult situations. This approach applied in governors' meetings when he would sometimes ask challenging questions, usually of the Education Office's representatives, but also often of me. We were certainly kept on our toes as he made us think and question. He also helped us to move forward without losing sight of our, or his principles, and this, I believe, is the basis of any good antiracist work. It was a delight to see the confidence of the Governing body grow under his chairmanship – and there was always a good attendance.

Involvement in School

Barry took his governorship seriously and saw the responsibility to involve more than attending meetings: he wanted to see, and take part in, the daily routine of the school. He soon became well known and his greeting, 'Wotcha?!' was addressed to us all. It didn't matter whether it was me, the caretaker, a parent or a child, we were all treated with the same esteem. No-one got special treatment, but everyone felt special.

It was, however, his work with pupils that he enjoyed the most. This was his opportunity to put theory into practice and he spent time talking and working with pupils around issues of racism and prejudice. As well as enabling him to develop his own thinking, the pupils gained a great deal from these sessions in which they were challenged to think and to question. The youngsters took readily to him and he became affectionately known as 'BT'. It was at this time, in 1992, that John Major stated at the Conservative Party Conference, that 'primary teachers should learn how to teach children to read, not waste their time on the politics of gender, 'race' and class'. There was no argument with the first part of the statement but none of us could agree that work in our area of gender, 'race' and class was a waste of time. As 90% of the pupils belonged to minority ethnic groups, mainly of Indian or Pakistani origin, and many did not have English as their first language, we felt that it was particularly important to make time for this work. Thus, the school's Equal Opportunity Policy, and the decision to apply for a 'determination' to exempt the school from the legal requirement to hold a 'broadly Christian' act of collective worship, were areas that we, and Barry, were actively involved in.

Barry also accompanied staff and pupils on residential visits, taking his turn with responsibilities and finding out how exhausting, but also how rewarding, such experiences can be. In addition, he was a regular attender on our annual Family outings to the seaside. These were events when, on a chosen Saturday in July, coaches would leave the school laden with children, parents, grandparents, aunts, uncles, and anyone else who wanted to come, off to spend a day at the coast. On one memorable occasion a coach broke down on the way home from Brighton. Barry was there with a couple of the dads, at the side of the motorway, sleeves rolled up, trying to get the coach started. The passengers were most impressed! On another trip to Skegness Barry brought his own family along, his dad and his wife Sally. They too had become part of the school.

Being a governor, and the Chair in particular, wasn't always easy for Barry. There were times when hard decisions had to be made. Perhaps the most difficult task that he was involved in was the redeployment of a member of staff. LMS was hitting hard and budgetary difficulties resulted in the need to make substantial savings. The most effective way to do this was by losing a member of the teaching staff despite the tremendous implications for the school as a whole. This was a time when the full reality of being a governor became all too painfully clear and people looked to Barry, as Chair, for guidance.

By this time Barry had become a member of the staffroom and had formed many good relationships. Staff liked, and respected him and there was always a great deal of laughter when he was around. This task, therefore, did not sit well. The governing body set about their awful job in a professional and fair way: which did not, however, make things any easier. The fact that the governors knew staff as people complicated matters, but perhaps that was right. Losing someone who has been part of a team should never be easy, and it wasn't. Barry agonised with the rest of us. At a later date he wrote in the 'Preface' to *Racism and Education*, (1993) 'it is dispiriting, to say the least, to witness the strains of teaching and learning in an under-resourced, undervalued, often demonised educational system'.

Barry's Legacy

Barry's last involvement with the school before his illness, was at a training session for staff and governors. This session was spent in evaluating the school's achievements and in looking to the future. During the evening two of the governors, a female Sikh parent governor and a male, Muslim LEA nominee, agreed to take on the roles of Chair and Vice-Chair. Both of them had attended the school as pupils! Barry's support had undoubtedly enabled them to feel confident in taking on responsibility, and he had achieved his aim.

A year on from his death the school, and the Governing body are still grieving. Barry has, however, left his mark on us all. For example: Barry was always opposed to 'League Tables' of schools. He felt strongly that they did not give a true picture of schools' or pupils' achievements, especially when many of the pupils had English as an additional language. In July, 1996, the governors took a stance by refusing to submit the results of the Key Stage 2 SATs results to the Department for Education and Employment. In effect they were breaking the law. This was a brave step which could not have been taken without the political and educational philosophy that Barry had provided and, in a way the decision was a tribute to him. There was only one kind of league table that had any meaning to Barry and yes, we still look out for the Spurs' results!

The school is due to be inspected by OFSTED in 1997. Although the Framework for the Inspection of Schools contains no direct reference to antiracist education, there is mention of equal opportunities: a slightly different perspective from that of John Major in 1992. The school feels secure that Barry's work in, and commitment to, this area, both in his professional and personal life has, without a doubt, inspired us and taken us forward. Our inspection will be a celebration of our work and relationship with Barry. What we will miss though, is the opportunity to observe his relationship with the inspectors.

The Future

Schools move on and have to look to the future. A Conservative government of 18 years duration undoubtedly had an enormous impact on schools and on the work that Barry so passionately believed in. What perspective the new Labour government will take on antiracist work is not clear. It is interesting though, that many schools remain firmly committed to it. Some of this commitment is, I believe, directly attributable to Barry's writings, and to his work with student teachers who have gone out and 'spread the word'. This is certainly the case for our staff and governors. Barry's support through the last period of change has no doubt equipped us to confront, challenge, and have the strength to do what we feel is in the best interests of our pupils, parents, and the local community.

Barry's wife, Sally, has recently become one of our governors. Work on developing a wildlife garden, begun when Barry was the Chair, is nearing completion and a decision to plant a tree in his memory has been taken. This will be a fitting memorial to someone who enabled us all to grow and develop through our association with him.

Reference

Troyna, B. (1993) *Racism and Education* Buckingham, Open University Press

7

HOLDING ON TOGETHER: CONVERSATIONS WITH BARRY

Ivor Goodson

I have been thinking a lot about Barry recently. My guess is that re-entering British society after a number of years in North America has intensified some of these engagements. To re-enter is to once again encounter the finely-grained nuances and calibrations of an obsolescent class system. In examining the dress code and accent of each individual person you have the best indicator of class location and of the various resistances and loyalties that are embedded in this social structure. Barry Troyna's dress code was a mixture of avid Spurs supporter 'up for the cup' and rapacious street punk. Likewise his accent and his speech reflected the argot of the Spurs' terraces. It was genuinely as if he had never been away.

In contradiction to the North American working class that I leave behind, pockets of English life still represent some of the resiliences and resistances that have been polished over many centuries. At its best, and of course I romanticise, the dress coding and argot of working class life can still capture the chirpiness, the carnivalesque elements of an enduring culture. To use a phrase of the moment, it is to have some experience of the '*flaneur*'. What did this mean in the case of Barry? He knew full well that his appearance and language carried a cost in terms of his acceptance into the higher reaches of English professional society. So, was it simply a romantic yearning back, or holding on, to some mythical golden age of East End working class life? Or could there have been some intellectual and political purpose behind the ubiquitous jeans, feathered haircut and rhyming slang? Having talked in some detail with him about this, and sharing some 'insider knowledge', it is perfectly clear to me that it was the latter. Barry was committed to the emancipation and empowerment of historically and structurally disadvantaged groups in British society and 'holding on', as he did, in spite, or because of, the personal 'cost', was part of a succinct, specific and political life project to refine and reflect resistances, resiliences, and loyalties. He wanted to give something back.

In this chapter I want to focus on Barry's concerns about the part that research might or might not play in the empowerment and emancipation of disadvantaged groups. I was lucky in that, in his last two years we spent a good deal of time working on a life history project in Canada which was particularly concerned to examine the potential for life history with regard to the education of racial ethnocultural minorities (a project funded by the Social Science and Humanities Research Council of Canada).

Barry was enthusiastic about life history approaches and had used them both as a teaching strategy and in research. Nevertheless, questioning taken for granted assumptions and conventional wisdoms, always making everything problematic was ever his way and he had some important epistemological and ethical questions to ask about life history. In particular he was concerned, and it has to be said, sceptical, about claims that individuals and groups can achieve some degree of empowerment and emancipation through use of the methodology. Fortunately, some of the conversations that we had about these issues were recorded enabling me, to some extent, to revisit and reappraise the kinds of things that we were mutually exploring. Returning to a transcript of a tape also gives an opportunity to 'see' Barry at work as an interviewer and, in however slight a way, to recapture a sense of the man himself.

We began by talking about life history interviewing:

BT: We spoke a bit about the interview itself.... and you reckon that you choose to be fairly passive, fairly recessive. Two questions arising from that. Firstly, can you give me a justification?... and, ...is that the routine start? Are there any situations in which you would change that?

IG: Taking that in reverse order, I guess there would always be situations where I would change being a reflexive researcher (ha, ha). But in terms of being passive, that's the question of my analysis of the stages that one goes through in an interview for life history; so whilst I would start passive, I would think one would get more and more active as the process went through. So we talked a bit last week about these three stages which are not discreet, but which I believe exist, which begin with a more passive attempt to elicit what I call the raw narration of the life story from the life story teller which of course isn't raw but which is a script coming from them without much prompting. So, in that sense, the interview is passive in that first period where they're eliciting that prime narration, the first narration, a kind of script to the life, but then there would be some more stages which I describe as collaboration and location where you would ask a series of questions about that first narration of the life story which seemed to locate it, challenge it and interrogate it and position it, sociologically and historically.

BT: So it would become progressively focused?

IG: Yeah, progressively focused and progressively more interactive I think to be honest with you. Progressively, I would prefer to say, collaborative.

BT: What happens if your respondent... didn't want the interactive relationship that you request?

IG: You mean all you get is just their first telling of their life script? Well, all you've got is their first telling of the life script.

BT: Does this undermine the whole enterprise for you?

IG: Not necessarily but I mean, obviously, you have to deal with that as it is which is something where you haven't had any chance to seriously interact or question or locate as I call it, and so it would be of limited use and it would be particularly of limited use for me because I see the collaboration around that initial life story as a crucial piece of collaborative research and investigation and what works. That seems to me that the very important stage for me in trying to get some sort of collaborative 'trade' going with the life story teller otherwise, I mean, they end up with exactly the knowledge of their life that they first had and their understanding hasn't been broadened in some sense as mine hasn't either. So the collaboration around that first telling of the life story script is a crucial trading point for research, understanding, investigation, theory building, whatever that collaborative pact that we develop with the life story teller is.....

BT: Why would they want (their) understanding of their lives to be enhanced by you?

IG: I'm not saying it would be enhanced by me. I think it would be enhanced collaboratively: a simple distinction. Why would they want me to be part of their enhanced understanding, to rephrase you? Well, because I think it's often useful for some people, sometimes, to have another person or another presence while they work through and, in fact, another position, if you will, somebody standing there in an alternative position involving them in a conversation about their life. Some people would want that conversation, some wouldn't, so I think the question of why would people want enhanced understanding is obviously a key question. Some people do and some people don't. My business has tended to be to try to help people broaden their understanding of themselves, but that's just my purpose, but I would want to work with people who had that as a belief that they wanted to pursue, that they want to come to understand their life, their life history, better. I would imagine that I wouldn't be working collaboratively with people who didn't because, clearly, they wouldn't collaborate, I wouldn't want to....

BT: So at the initial stage of the life history enterprise, you would explain in detail what is required of these people? What their commitment should be? What your role is?

IG: Yeah, I don't know whether I would is the truth...... laying out in detail what the collaboration is about is actually jumping the gun. Because... many people might not want to go to stage two... and they have the right not to. So if you from the beginning define this as something which is about enhancing their understanding or working with them towards understanding, which is the way I prefer to put it, you're kind of pre-judging immediately the kind of person that you are seeking and the kind of collaboration you are seeking. Obviously, there are as many positions on this as there are people. And I think it is perfectly legitimate to say, as some people have, actually, 'look, I've told you my life story, that's enough, I don't want to know any more', that doesn't invalidate that particular rendition that you've got, it is a life story which you have not been able to collaborate around, but it is still a life story.

BT: Does it still retain the properties of the life history interview?

IG: No, not at all, because the crucial distinction to grasp for me, is the distinction between life story and life history. The life story, as I understand it, is the version of events that you render to me over time. Your partial, selective story. It is a story and we all have one.. and we would tell different stories at different times in our life. The life history would seek to position and locate that story by bringing in other data, other insights, other theories, other questions which have not been raised in the initial rendition of the story... You would move from story to life history by, in my case, that crucial, intermediary, collaborative act which brings in other data and other questions to try and locate the quotes of the life story and.. render it a life history.

BT: OK. The way that you described it is as a collaborative enterprise, ultimately and ideally. What I've not got is any sense of it being an interactive enterprise. There's Ivor Goodson coming in and getting all this information from people... but Ivor Goodson is still the shadowy figure who is defined pure and simple by his status as a researcher.. Why should I trust you? Why should anyone trust you? What are you going to give to us?

IG: I don't think I can answer that theoretically. You see, I think the question about who collaborates with whom and why they do it is... a deeply personal one. Often to do with eye contact, body language, chemistry, background, a million things which are quite impossible to legislate or predict so there is no answer in a vacuum to what you say. All that I can say is that some people at some times have trusted me, and I don't quite know why. I can certainly list a number of things that the shadowy researcher, as you described me, might bring to this trade, this collaborative action, which would be a whole range of different kinds of thoughts and insights about life stories over time and about school histories and curriculum histories....

BT: Is there any way that we, as researchers, can expedite the success with that relationship so that, for instance... the researcher would provide you with a research biography? Would you go along with that?

IG: Yes, I think I would. I mean, one of the things that I deeply believe in as part of the collaborative conversation that follows the initial kind of unmediated narration of the life story, is a lot of exchange around the life story, the researcher and the life story of the life story teller. So I would nearly always in my conversation, in that conversation, in the collaborative second stage, bring in quite a bit of information about my own biography.

BT: I have a problem... It is a problem with this whole issue of reflexivity... which is, how would you describe this process? You put a great deal of emphasis on one's own personal resources, being intuitive, 'duck and dive' when necessary, the development of certain tactics which are appropriate here, but not there, and so on. How does this coalesce around the methodology; how can you package this as a methodology which others can learn from? It seems there's a whole array of different and individualised tactics.

IG: Yeah, I think that's an extremely good question for which I don't have an answer.... Rather than doing what I think implicitly most people want us to do which is, as you say, your phrase, 'how do we package your methodology?', I think that there are some methodologies which are frankly unpackageable because... personal dynamics are themselves unpackageable.

BT: OK. If I accept that method, which I do, then you can't socialise the young, inexperienced researcher and that's one of my reservations about it. But given all of that, do you think that it was precipitous and ill advised to go into a project, such as this one, where the whole idiosyncratic model is overladen with a whole range of new problems, namely for power, asymmetry?

IG: Yeah, maybe. But how would you suspend or solve those problems with any other methodology?

BT: Depends what you specify as the problems. But I think that those problems are exacerbated with this where one is acting as a therapist, more or less, asking deeply personal, potentially incredibly intrusive questions of individuals whose position within the society is highly vulnerable.

IG: But what's the logical conclusion for that if you are asking difficult questions of people? Not to ask them? Not to speak to them about it? What's your alternative? Silence?

BT: Well, one of the arguments which goes on in race relations research is, the focus shouldn't be on the black community, the focus should be on racism. How would you respond to that?

IG: No, I think it is a legitimate question, but you can see what I'm saying and it comes back to whether.... we exacerbate questions by talking to people and questioning people about things, or whether we help create the flow of dialogue around perilous and problematic issues, and I think a lot of that cannot be prejudged. I think it depends on the way it's done. I don't inevitably always think that asking difficult questions of people, even if they are, as in some case, as is quite rightly the case here, in subordinate positions, that inevitably these invoke some form of colonising or genome or whatever you want to call it. It depends on the form of the collaboration, the form of the trust, to use your phrase, and the form of the trade..... it would be wrong, I think, to say across the board.... if you ask difficult questions of people who are differentially located in the power structure (it) inevitably exacerbates their situation. I don't think it does inevitably exacerbate. It might, on the other hand, it might actually help and enhance their understanding of their situation..... So it all depends on the nature of the conversation and the dialogue and the form it takes. It might exacerbate or it might enhance.

BT: I guess I'm dubious that it could ever enhance and I'm dubious because I don't believe in the empowering properties of research. I think it's a grandiose and disingenuous conception of social and educational research which has been perpetuated from, reproduced mainly for the benefit of, the social and educational researchers.

IG: I'll buy that.... which is why we are now talking about the form of research which certainly has properties behind that – which is certainly attempted to engage in more everyday life kind of conversational forms of research... You may well be right that any form of interaction across such power divides inevitably exacerbates. I would be reluctant to accept that. I think that even if, if we for a moment could conceive of less grandiose forms of research, and I would hope that in some ways this might be one route to that, I would be reluctant to think that conversations across power divides could not enhance understanding because that would mean simply that groups can't talk to each other in any meaningful ways.

BT: Understandings of what? Understandings that they are members of oppressed groups?

IG: Well no. Let's push it a bit more. What about if, for example, let's take teachers and let's for a moment think of them as an oppressed group, which certainly some people would argue they are and certainly they have some properties of an oppressed group. Let's for a minute imagine that the kind of conversations around life history, around studying the teacher's life and work, led teachers to have much more vivid and cognitive maps of the groups of people that influence them, of the groups of people that oppressed them, and the groups of the sort of strategies that might work against those oppressive practices. And if those cognitive maps of resisting oppression or of understanding how oppressions are administered came out of the conversation that we are talking about, I would think that might enhance teachers' understanding of the world in which they live and work. I would think that would be a good thing.

BT: It's a liberal humanist position to adopt isn't it? They are all dressed up, to use Meatloaf's phrase, they are all dressed up with no place to go. OK. So now they know that the world is an oppressive place in which they live and there are certain things that have gone on in their life which have accentuated their vulnerability. What would you do about it?

IG: Mine might be a little humanist, yours sounds unduly determinist in the sense that.... to pursue the argument that when people have a better understanding of how they might politically and actively work for a better world, is meaningless. Is to cut up almost any possibility in action. Is that what you are doing?

BT: No. What I'm saying is that the life history methodology, with it's highly individualised focus, doesn't actually prepare the ground very well for collective action.... (although) I think the collective subject scenario... has a lot more potential and it's certainly the approach I would want to support.

IG: But, I think one of the great advantages of the one on one, essentially individualistic mode... is that in quiet corners a couple of people can have conversations about these various things which allow both of them to try out ideas that they can later try out in more collective scenarios. And that's what we, as your unspeakable researchers do, all the time...

BT: The possibility then from either collective or individualistic life history is resistance. Is a recognition of what's going on and generation of activities to deal with those sorts of oppression on this project. That's a possibility (but) the reality is that Professor Ivor Goodson will go to New Orleans and Kings College, London, and here, there and everywhere to talk about this research. That's the reality. There is an inevitability about that that may be over determined. How would you respond to the claim, therefore, that, that to use perhaps an indelicate phrase of Patti Lather, you are simply involved in 'rape research'?....

IG: It's obviously quite conceivable that this could be presented as 'rape research' in a sense that, yes, I have these conversations and then I go off to other arenas and talk to different audiences, in different ways about these things. But it begs the question of what I do in these other audiences and other places. If I thought that I gave addresses which presented the people I've talked to in an unwitting and unwilling light, then yes, that would obviously be a prime case of rape 'research', but it begs the question very much, of what I talk about. As a matter of fact, I never talked about anyone's life history in the places that you've just talked about. So I never talk about those personal histories in a personal way in those places. I do talk about the methodological and ethical issues that they raise and the possibility that this may be 'rape research', but then that's something that I should talk about and it's important to talk about in those hallowed halls of the academy. But, I mean, all I'm saying is that it begs the question of how one talks about this research in other places. One might talk about it in a way that does confirm the allegation of 'rape research', or one might talk about it in ways that raise issues which in some sense resonate with the concerns of the prior collaborative life history work. So it may or may not be exploitative.

BT: But the rhetoric still remains, doesn't it, in so far as you talk in terms of the three stages of narration, collaboration, location and hope that with the subject you will achieve those goals. You can go through those stages and achieve it. That's the ambition, that's the aspiration and it may or may not happen. What will happen is that ultimately you have responsibility, the research team has the responsibility for selecting, filtering and representing that person's life in the academy, either personally through being invited to talk in New Orleans, or through the written word of an article in the Journal of Education Policy or whatever. So there is no doubt whatsoever that you will benefit as a researcher from this activity. There is some doubt that the life history teller will benefit. That's more dubious.

IG: Absolutely true.

BT: OK, if you accept that, is it morally reprehensible to engage black people in this project, given your own hegemonic position as a white, male, Professor?

IG: For a white project on black people?

BT: Yeah, that's right, I don't want to develop a hierarchy of oppression... Well, maybe I would focus on black people because it is well documented... in the literature.

IG: But what you are asking is a question that seems to me to move beyond blackness.

BT: Yeah

IG: This is a question about researchers, privileged researchers in this case, dealing with groups at other levels of their hierarchy, normally subordinate positions. I don't know. I don't know how you resolve that..... I've just done a summer school where I was doing life history work with principals and administrators who are, I think you'd admit, a less oppressed group than some of the groups of teachers we've been talking about. By researching upwards you turn some of these issues on their heads, but that isn't the way out of the problem. I mean the issue is if you are researching or conversing with, or however you want to present the relationship, oppressed groups, you are implicated in the differential power structures of society. But frankly I can't see any way that you could suspend that. You can either try and deal with it and seek not to exacerbate it and to confront and to find strategies that resist it in your work as far as you can, but you are still, since you are located in a power structure, you are still implicated. And you are as well as them.

BT: Oh yeah, sure... Let's go to this researching upwards issue which I think is a very interesting one. You said earlier that what's in it for them, the life history teller, is the possibility of, to use your term, empowerment, collective action, bla, bla, bla. What's in it for the elite? Why should the elite have you peril his life story?

IG: I don't know, but sometimes they do......

BT: OK, so if from this project you had two or three appointments with life history tellers and the issue of ethnicity, racism did not emerge, would that not prove troublesome to you?

IG: I think it would not worry me at all if it didn't emerge in the, what I call, early stages of narration of the script. It would worry me enormously if in the interactive collaboration and the discussion it wasn't raised because I would expect to raise it... One of my questions in that next phase would be, 'OK, you've told me your life story but I don't have any sense of you as a black man and that is what I see in front of me, why is that?' So yeah, I would pose it in that form, but the important point to grasp is, I would be posing that question in a very different way to the way we talked about using it yesterday. Where you go in and say, 'OK, you're a black man, tell me about it'. One way you'd obviously get that, the other way, you've got a longer run at the issue and I much prefer my strategy to yours.

BT: ....But the issue didn't come up with Walter (*one of the life story tellers in Ivor's project*)

IG: It didn't with Walter yet... but that's not over yet.

BT: But that's 300 pages (*of transcript*)!

IG: Yes that's 300 pages but what we've still got to do.... is go back and raise a lot of other issues about location..... Walter and I need a conversation about that before we push at some new questions.

BT: How would you respond to the observation that what this project is doing is strengthening the sense of otherness? A tendency that characterises race relations research, where decontextualising black people from the normal conceptualisation of the teacher identifying the others as odd, different or deviant while naturalising whites in that role. How would you respond to that?

IG: I think I would respond with a counter to you which is to say that by going out and pushing from the beginning to blackness and other issues, you're doing that.

BT: I'm responding to a research agenda in a tactical way. The research agenda has been set by you and your colleagues and that research agenda differentiates black teachers from others.

IG: Yeah, but you see, in some ways you want it both ways there. Which is that you're saying that you want us to get at this sense of otherness and that it hasn't come out yet, and then you are turning around and telling me that I'm strengthening their sense of otherness. You can't have it both ways. The truth is, I think, we've tried in ways that are not always successful, I would accept that, to try and deal with the question of otherness, which is undoubtedly there with any of them, whether that be a racial other or an other, other we've tried to deal with that in ways that give a reasonable degree of voice to the beginning, to the person, to phrase that particular question as they will themselves. Now that doesn't get me off the hook of otherness but it allows the otherness to be dealt with by them, rather than from day one by you when you go straight in and say, 'OK, tell me...' No, I don't think either of those solves the problem of how we've researched otherness. They are just two different ways of going at it, I think. And I wouldn't, I think, claim priority for this method but I think it's at least a sustainable way of approaching a considerable problem in our society.

So there it is, a slice of conversation with Barry. Returning to the interview confirms my absolute sense of loss: for 'holding on' to roots is a process that requires constant re-affirmation from valued friends. Defending any sense of equalitarian projects in the past eighteen years in England has been a perilous and problematic process. Let us hope that the Labour victory of May 1st truly heralds a new dawn. I know for sure that is what Barry would be hoping.

As you read this transcript it is impossible not to appreciate the power and inquisitiveness of his mind – his questions are un-negotiated, direct and full-frontal. There is none of the fudging and hedging, the searching for the acceptable question that is so much part of English professorial life. I once asked him what he hated most about being an academic. His answer was immediate, 'the ducking and diving, twisting and turning to avoid confronting issues directly'. He had no time for this. He wanted to 'tell it straight'. But to tell it straight in English academic life is to pay a huge price, especially if you look like a Spurs supporter out on the town, or, as someone so famously once put it, 'a sulky boy in denims'. The professorial community tends to close ranks against the alien outsider in a way that reminds me of Erving Goffman's (1963) study of Stigma. The focus is moved to the unacceptable 'style' of the person – which is judged to be 'non-professorial'. Thus the content of their intellectual work is neatly side-stepped and the challenge of that work and line of inquiry, effectively stymied. This is the true and appalling legacy of the intersection between English class society and professorial life. Nobody reading this transcript could doubt Barry's brilliance but so often the audience concentrated on his style, his otherness.

He judged this a price worth paying – to make the essential and obvious point: it is not how you dress or talk that has anything to do with your intellect or worth. The badge of the class society has nothing to do with the badges of self-worth. In an iconic way Barry's life and work proves this essential point.

References

Goffman, E. (1963) *Stigma: Notes on the Management of Spoiled Identity*, Englewood Cliffs, Prentice Hall

8

FROM THE STREETS OF TOTTENHAM TO ANTIPODEAN SOUTH AUSTRALIA: SEDUCTIONS AND DILEMMAS IN THE TRAVELS OF ANTIRACISM

VICKI CROWLEY

Recently while searching for some teaching texts on masculinities I came across a chapter by Frank Mort which began,

> Imagine yourself on Tottenham High Road on a winter Saturday afternoon. The pavements are blocked, but not with Christmas shoppers. A continuous stream of male youth are making for the Spurs ground. Look once and it might have been the rituals of class played out unchanged since the 1950s. Look again. It is 1987, not 1957. What has changed are the surfaces of the lads themselves, the ways they carry their masculinity. Individuality is on offer, incited through commodities and consumer display. From jeans: red tabs, designer labels, distressed denim. To hair: wedges, spiked with gel, or pretty hard boys who wear it long, set off with large earring. And the snatches of boy's talk I pick up about 'looking wicked' as well as the game. Which is not to say the violence is designer label! (1988, p.193)

I was immediately transported into a world enjoyed by Barry Troyna, just as I was immediately reminded of venturing with him to a Spurs home game in the late winter of 1993. Unlike the seamless populace that captures Mort's imagination, my remembering of Tottenham High Road and a Spurs game is one of a much more diverse populace troubled and interpreted by the gaze of a traveller and tourist. More than just being reminded of streetscape and popular culture, however, Mort's passage reminds me of a sense of incongruity and curiosity – a structure of feeling (Williams, 1979), that is a persistent presence in my reading and use of Troyna's work. It is a structure of feeling that accompanies seeing one thing and reading another, about the fissures between author, text, and worlds that inform and perhaps pervade what is written despite their apparent absence.

My feet on the pavements of Tottenham High Road, however, were not merely those of traveller and tourist but also those of student and teacher puzzling over the representations, discursive practices and actualities (Grossberg, 1993) of racism and antiracism.

Looking at soccer in the flesh and in the company of an avid supporter is quite different to looking at soccer on late night television in an Australian living room. The trajectories of racism and the politics and practices of antiracism are not the same for either visiting, or local theorist. Reading soccer, reading racism and antiracism are neither static, nor gender neutral practices. Yet all are serviced by discourses that make deciphering context and content possible.

Being on Tottenham High Road was not the first time I had pondered issues of reading theory, popular politics, the writing subject and writing the subject in relation to Troyna's work. Indeed, the very first time I heard Troyna give a paper in Adelaide I was struck by his twinned response of resisting commentary on the unfamiliar and an insistence on locating his analysis in the British context. Across these responses, I was also struck by the seductions of a theoretical universalism that so often insidiously accompanies popular politics such as antiracism. Thus, it is no mere mention or moment of whimsy that I refer to Tottenham High Road. for, as Mort intended[1], his description of Tottenham High Road brings to life tensions of scholar, scholarship, popular politics and theory.

A relationship with street and streetscape, tenacious loyalties and political desire fuel Troyna's educational work on antiracism.

Indeed, his work is irrevocably grounded in such terrains. For a number of reasons, including scepticism regarding postmodernism, however, Troyna, did not foreground these kinds of relationships in his work. I am not so much concerned with Troyna's absenting of his own subjectivity but rather it is some of the tensions created by the absence of these relationships that holds my attention and flags the interrogatory directions that I take from his work. This begins to suggest that it is often as much in departure and concomitance that the influence and power of an author's work is to be appreciated and measured. Ideas are formed across paradox and contradiction, and thus, in a Lacanian sense perhaps, it is as much through what Troyna's work is, and what it is not, that for me opens a creative dialogue. This is especially so as I think across the travel of theory and the discourses and discursive practices of antiracism.

James Clifford and Vivek Dhareshwar write that,

> Theory, by definition, is more than a local act. While it is enmeshed in specific traditions and locales, and while it is marked by the site and condition of its production, its purview is extensive, generalising, comparative. If theories no longer totalise, they do travel. Indeed, in their diverse rootings and uprootings, theories are constantly translated, appropriated, contested, grafted. Theory travels; so do theorists... This very mobility and movement gives rise to unresolved questions, in need of systematic examination. (1989, p.vii)

It is to the dilemmas over the travel of theory[2], that have shaped the directions I have taken with Troyna's work, to which I want now to turn. This is not so much to subject them, in this instance, to systematic examination, but to note sites of tension and dilemma that emerge for me out of an engagement with elements of Troyna's work and the sense of curiosity and incongruity that seems to always accompany it.

Some journeys with antiracism

There are two key moments in Troyna's mid to late 80s work that persist in being unsettling and baffling to me, impelling, perhaps, the sense of curiosity and incongruity that so pervades my engagement with his work. The provocatively titled paper *'Whose side are we on?' Ethical dilemmas in research on 'race' and education'* (co-authored with Bruce Carrington, 1989), and use of the couplet 'racism and sexism', represent currents that haunt and niggle at my work. They are, for me, sites of unresolved dilemma, both within and of themselves and as mutually constitutive constructs that hold a certain taken-for-grantedness in the popular politics of antiracism. Dilemmas, as Billig *et al.* (1988) suggest, and after whom Troyna deployed the term, concern contrary notions and contain presuppositions. Indeed Troyna's deployment of 'Whose side are we on?' and 'racism and sexism' are interventions in dilemmas he saw as facing antiracism, pedagogy and research. Like all concepts, terms and theory, they contain a series of presuppositions that establish a directional focus and field of vision.

For Troyna the question of 'Whose side are we on?' is situated in the vexed politics of doing 'ethical' research that empowers, rather than disempowers the researched. The question of 'Whose side are we on?' is settled in a call for reflexive research that is committed to 'values' rather than 'factions' (Gouldner in Troyna and Carrington, 1989). Yet the question of 'Whose side are we?' is one that lingers long after its situationally located treatment. For me, it is the category 'we' that is a particular and ongoing site of disturbance. This is, in part, because it is presupposed by an imagined and harmonious group of researchers and antiracist activists. It also presupposes a continuity between subject and content. It is thus not the superficial essentialism of the category that is the problem, but the affiliative connections with, assumptions about, and the encapsulation of racism and antiracism as if these are fully known and fixed entities rather than a vexed *mélange* of conflicted and mobile workings. These presuppositions also assist a certain taken-for-grantedness in the 'anti' of antiracism – an anti that is certain about who and what is being opposed. In turn, it often contains a taken-for-grantedness that the discourses of popular and educational antiracism do not re-inscribe racism. And, while we might, for instance, be familiar with the theoretical and political trajectories of a weak multiculturalism, racism awareness training, and cultural sensitivity, (Troyna and Williams, 1986) we might be less familiar with the everyday explanations of racism that are brought to explain the logics and project of antiracism – explanations whose tendrils reach back to the explanatory frameworks of racism. These presuppositions militate against a reflexive practice that interrogates the resources and strategies that antiracism itself brings to racism, just as it keeps alive recourse to narrow representations of racism. They propel a directional focus and field of vision that is in danger of being unable to grapple with the grafting of antiracism from racism and the mobility of racism, its remakings and shifting articulations.

The question of 'Whose side are we on?' also dances in close proximity to the more vigorous and invidious question of 'Whose side are you on?'. Indeed, inside the actualities of racism and the politics of antiracism the 'we' easily becomes one of 'you' as, for instance, in the much publicised events of the murder of Ahmed Iqbal Ullah (Macdonald *et al.*, 1989) or the Thomas Hill/Anita Clarence Affair (Morrison, 1992). A presupposition, even imprimatur, of the location of 'we' and 'you' is the issue of loyalty. It is not that I want to suggest that loyalties are not important. Rather, I want to suggest that loyalties are not sacrosanct and might not be singularly determined. The slippage into loyalties and universalised categories raises a series of issues that require continuous examination and re-examination. We might repeatedly need to ask: What kinds of arguments and discourses are brought into play to settle the question of sides? We might also ask: What of the notion of multi-accented subjectivities (McCarthy, 1990, p. 10), or to use Trinh Minh-ha's term, 'hyphenated identities and hybrid realities' (1991, p. 73)?

The issue of complex subjectivity brings me to Troyna's deployment of 'racism and sexism'. It is a couplet that presents an enormous raft of issues, none the least of which occurs in the presuppositions of equivalence, or for instance, in the context of poststructuralist and postcolonial feminist theory. These suggest a breadth of dilemmas beyond the bounds of this chapter. Like the question of 'Whose side are we on?', it is however, a notion deeply embedded in a particular kind of political struggle. It is a political struggle which is, in part, a desire on Troyna's part, to recognise the multiplicity of oppressions. It also arises in Troyna's work from a desire to neither privilege nor disprivilege one form of oppression over another. It is, however, a couplet that suggests distinct trajectories while it simultaneously notes at least some overlapping axes of oppression (Caraway, 1991), and- at best reading- a site of some indivisibility. In Troyna's mid 80s, early 90s work it is unequivocally, however, a moment that presupposes the centrality and giveness of class as a structuring force in social and cultural relations.

I do not eschew the materiality of class or the resources a class analysis can bring to racism, but, not dissimilarly to the question of 'Whose side are we on?', it represents a series of presuppositions that construct a field of vision supporting the continuation of a political project that is largely uninterrupted by questions of hybridity. It creates a field of vision that avoids deep fissures and incongruities while, ironically, it draws attention to a deep ambivalence around questions of masculinities, femininities and sexualities. Troyna's later work displays a broadening of the couplet of racism and sexism towards the salience of 'gender' in educational work on racism and antiracism (see for instance Troyna and Vincent, 1995). It is, however, an acknowledgement of the absence of gender in his work rather than a move towards a complexly inflected reading of racism.

When considering the issue of subjectivity, writing the subject, cultural contexts, and political interventions, the provocativeness and niggling of the question of 'Whose side are we on?', and the questions raised by the couplet of 'racism and sexism' combine to suggest research possibilities that are complex and unsettled. Let me bring this to life with a brief example from a recent research project. It is a research project in which I interviewed a series of antiracist educators, many of whom were responsible for the design and implementation of the South Australian Education Department's Antiracism Policy. I asked people to tell how they came to antiracism and came to recognise racism. Like many interviews, the storying travelled far and wide. One story, however, involved an adult man recounting and reliving his childhood experiences as family 'translator'. In particular he told of having to translate between a gynaecologist and his mother. She had trouble with her pregnancies and wanted to know why. In abrasive and hostile terms, the gynaecologist accused her of stupidity because she'd had a hysterectomy when she had given birth to her son – a procedure of which she was totally unaware. The gynaecologist drew diagrams for the young boy who endured a myriad of emotions including his mothers distress and humiliation, that spilled in many directions.

In some, perhaps many senses, this is both a familiar and an unfamiliar story. In the discourses of racism and antiracism, however, it is most often the kind of story told to exemplify the excess, horrors and abuse of racism. Yet it is so much more. It brings into play loyalties, oppositions, questions of subjectivity: issues beyond a man telling a story, and beyond racism and antiracism as some unidirectional school based project.

It most certainly is a powerful story. Its power derives from its insistent materiality and emotionality. It is also powerful because it ripples across many dilemmas of racism and antiracism, and in particular, it is powerful because the racialised subject speaks a shifting subjectivity across emotionality, embodiment, age, gender, life-stage, class, status 'knowing' – all of which is a refusal of fixity. It illustrates a subjectivity comprised of immersion in the knitted complexity of racialised and racialising gendered worlds, inflected by histories, power and vulnerabilities. It is across the surface and through the deeper tendrils of such a story that loyalties seem so abundantly apparent. But what happens when, moments later, the question of the gendering of women's experience of racism is expressly dismissed and the storying turns to racism read through the universality of masculinity, of men's stories in an uninflected world despite the immediacy of storying the contrary? How is it possible to tell one story at length and to then turn it away as one turns away from it? Part of an explanation lies in the constructions of the nature of the project, the privileging of some elements and stories over and above others. Part of an explanation lies in the split that is often policy and practice. Part lies in the available scripts for storying racism and antiracism. And part lies in the presuppositions of the discursive frameworks that construct the directional fields of vision. This brings to the fore 'that any sound strategy for researching racism must involve studying its expressions in its concrete material contexts', an insistence of Troyna's noted by Rizvi (1993, p.15). This links with a further maxim of Troyna's – a deeply interrogatory and reflexive practice is needed.

Subjectivity, culture and the travelling of theory

Across the disturbances of scholarly work, popular culture in its local contexts, puzzlement and resistance to a question of 'Whose side are we on?', the mobilisations of 'racism and sexism' and a sense of bafflement, curiosity and incongruity, is the absent presence (Morrison, 1990) of the always-already embodied and uneven subject. Its absence haunts the terrains on which antiracism is thought and practised. Its absence yields the irony that is the actuality of continuity between context and subject, and it is here that universalism works its seductions.

While Troyna and his work have travelled here and there, circulating in schools, in policy, in training, in university contexts; while it has been incorporated, criticised, rejected and refashioned, it most certainly contributes to the educational and schooling project of antiracism. Troyna's work provides a series of critical resources and tools for analysing the local across, but not exclusively in the shadow of the global, and brings into sharper view a series of terrains that contribute to the vitality of the project of antiracism.

I continue to keep an eye on Spurs on late night television and in the fine print of our sporting pages in the daily newspapers. Each time, as with Mort's description of Tottenham High Road, I am reminded of that complex and baffling nexus that is the writing subject and the subject written, of the uncanniness of worlds lived unevenly and texts written so seamlessly. I can only ever be left to ponder the nexus between the lad and older lad on Tottenham High Road and the passions that have driven his work. I most certainly would not have the resources and tools to 'think through' (Frankenburg, 1993) racism and antiracism without the contribution of Barry Troyna's work or the feisty engagement with it that it turns out to be. There is, however, no settlement or end in sight for this engagement. The question of 'Whose side are we on?', the vast residual problems of a couplet 'racism and sexism' and their mutually constitutive miasma, will continue to niggle at the edges of the work I do. As Clifford and Dhareshwar so aptly suggest, it is the very movement and mobility that give rise to 'unresolved questions' that are 'in need of systematic examination' (1989, p. vii). Thus it is as much in departure and concomitance that Troyna's work finds its way into mine to establish a series of questions that continue to so require systematic examination.

Notes

1. This is especially clear when Mort posits the question of 'Where do I stand in all this?' and contrasts himself to a generation that is not his own (1988:195).

2. The notion of travelling theory is far more complex than I endeavour to encounter here. In this instance I use the notion of travelling theory to suggest the journeys that I have taken with some elements of Troyna's work. They are journeys that occur because his work has travelled to Australia. The corpus of his work is read across a series of imagined contexts including imaginings about the location of its emergence, an uncritical application to the locations in which is read, and some analysis of the disjunctures that occur across site of emergence and site of reception. One disjuncture that is worth noting is that in South Australia, antiracism has waxed and waned as a site of popular politics with only a very recent resurgence that might in any way begin to resonate with its popular formations in Britain in the 1980s. Antiracism in education and schooling in South Australia is much more interventions of policy and bureaucracy than linkage or response to significant popular grassroots political activism.

References

Billig, M. *et al.* (1988) *Ideological Dilemmas,* London, Sage

Caraway, N. (1991) *Segregated Sisterhood,* Knoxville, University of Tennessee Press

Grossberg, L. (1992) *We Gotta Get Out Of This Place,* New York, Routledge

Macdonald, I., Bhavnani, T., Khan, L. and John, G. (1989) *Murder in the Playground: The Report of the Macdonald Inquiry into Racism and Racial Violence in Manchester Schools,* London, Longsight Press

McCarthy, C. (1990) *Race and Curriculum,* London, Falmer

Mort, F. (1988) 'Boy's Own? Masculinity, Style and Popular Culture', Chapman, R. and Rutherford, J. (Eds.) *Male Order: Unwrapping Masculinity,* London, Lawrence and Wishart, pp. 193-224

Frankenberg, R. (1993) *White Women, Race Matters,* Minneapolis, University of Minnesota Press

Morrison, T. (1990) *Playing in the Dark,* Cambridge, Massachusetts, Harvard University Press

Morrison, T. (Ed.) (1992) *Race-ing Justice, En-gendering Power,* New York, Pantheon

Rizvi, Fazal. (1993) 'Critical Introduction: Researching Racism and Education', Troyna, B. *Racism and Education,* Buckingham, Open University Press, pp.1-17

Trinh T. Minh-ha. (1991) *When the Moon Waxes Red,* New York, Routledge

Troyna, B. and Williams, J. (1986) *Racism Education and the State: The Racialisation of Education Policy*, London, Croom Helm

Troyna, B. (1987) 'A conceptual overview strategies to combat racist inequality in education: Introductory essay' Troyna, B. (Ed.) *Racial Inequality in Education,* London, Tavistock, pp.1-10

Troyna, B. and Carrington, B. (1989) 'Whose Side Are We On?': Ethical Dilemmas in Research on 'Race' and Education', Burgess, R.G. (Ed.) *Educational Research,* Falmer, London, pp. 205-223

Troyna, B. and Bruce Carrington, B. (1987) 'Antisexist/Antiracist Education – a False Dilemma: A Reply to Walkling and Brannigan', *Journal of Moral Education* 16, 1. pp. 60-65

Troyna, B. and Vincent, C. (1995) 'The Discourses of Social Justice in Education' *Discourse* 16, 2, pp.149-166

Williams, R. (1979) *Politics and Letters: Interviews with New Left Review,* London, New Left Books

9

RELATING EDUCATION POLICY AND INSTITUTIONALISED RACISM: FROM DISCOURSE TO STRUCTURE

Roger Dale

I first got to know Barry Troyna well when he visited New Zealand as part of his 'world tour' in 1991. I had been in New Zealand for less than two years at that time but it had already become evident that the area where my existing understandings of education systems were least useful, indeed misleading, was that of 'race relations' in education (though significantly, it was scarcely ever referred to in those terms there). The issue in Britain was framed by the social consequences of the legacy of Empire and the importation of cheap labour from poor countries. In the United States, the other country that we knew something about, the legacy of slavery was the central issue, though foreign labour was clearly of increasing importance. It was these two broad sets of problematics that underlay the issues around 'race and education', (though as I shall argue below, insufficiently explicitly).

By contrast, in New Zealand the main ethnic minority, comprising around 15% of the population, was the indigenous Maori people; the 'immigrants' were the colonising British. More than this, the minority culture was not in any sense a diasporic culture. There was no sense of 'home' being elsewhere, or dreams of return, or of the need to install the culture in an alien context. Maori culture exists only in New Zealand; if it dies in New Zealand it becomes extinct.

This is what made knowledge and understandings based on 'the West' unhelpful to the point of being misleading. What makes matters worse, and not only from a Maori point of view, is the attempt to apply those understandings as if their situation paralleled that reported and analysed in the northern hemisphere. Particularly for the Maori, such attempts were seen in themselves as perpetuating the forms of their oppression through education rather than as shedding light on it or showing the way forward. In particular, Maori educationists rejected the notion of multiculturalism, which would reduce Maori, the tangata whenua (the people of the land), to the status of just one minority culture among many. (For Maori interpretations of Maori education, and possible ways forward, see Mead, 1996; Smith, 1997; and Johnston (1997).

It was into this situation that Barry Troyna, a leading international expert in racism and racial inequality in education, came to deliver a series of seminars and conference papers in 1991. He was extremely well received and at the end of his short stay was invited to record a long interview for a Maori radio station. He neither patronised nor was patronised. He spoke trenchantly and was received with respect (a reaction that can by no means be guaranteed to speakers who come to Auckland and presume to tell Maori how to conduct their affairs, as several overseas experts have discovered). He was a popular and successful visitor who was well enough known and liked to make it important to announce the news of his death to a full staff meeting of the Education Department at Auckland University. He did not, of course, nor could he or anyone else expect to, dramatically change how these issues were viewed in New Zealand, though his critique of multiculturalism struck a positive note and is still referred to. Nor, as far as I have been able to ascertain, did his visit to New Zealand have any effect on his thinking about racism and education more generally.

He and I did, however, spend some time discussing how the differences apparent between New Zealand and Britain related to the broader issues of racism, education and the state. These discussions took place in the context of, but were not confined to, the book

Barry and Jenny Williams had published under that title a few years previously. At that time I was trying to work out how to theorise the relations between the state and racism and incorporate them in a more general theory of the state and its effects on education policy; I had considered using the notion of 'institutional racism' but had been put off somewhat by Barry and Jenny's powerful critique of its shortcomings; though, like them, I did hold on to the possibility that there might still be some mileage in the concept if it could be effectively refined.

I did not really follow up on those discussion, even, to my present surprise, in the paper that Barry asked me to present to the ESRC research seminar that he and David Halpin organised. In that paper I attempted explicitly to draw on the theoretical and methodological lessons I had drawn from the opportunity to compare two apparently similar but actually quite different education systems – but I did so without any reference to the issue of how racial or ethnic differences were defined and treated. Indeed, it was not until Pat and Fazal asked me to contribute to this volume that the extent of that omission came home to me. The main points I tried to make in that paper (which are elaborated in the version of part of it that appears in the volume on the ESRC seminar series that Barry and David edited; see Dale, 1994) was that the pressure to what I called 'premature application' of research findings in quick and easy 'solutions' was reinforcing pressures towards four undesirable theoretical short cuts: reliance on unstated ethnocentric assumptions; disciplinary parochialism; a focus on education politics rather than the wider politics of education that set the context in which education politics were played out; and a stress on problem-solving rather than critical theory. It now strikes me that assuming that the educational underachievement of Maori in New Zealand and Afro-Caribbeans in England can be understood, explained and remedied in the same way is the best possible example of where premature application can lead us. It also struck me that attempting to go beyond those shortcomings might be the best way that I could use this opportunity to develop Barry Troyna's work in the education policy field.

It is a major strength of Barry's work that it does not fall into the traps I have mentioned. For instance, the introduction to *Racism, Education and the State* (1986) is one of the best examples that can be found of the importance of placing education politics, in this case the detailed discussion of LEA policies, in the context of the broader politics of education. Similarly, the critique of institutional racism in the same book demonstrates the need to theoretically interrogate the quick fix, however superficially attractive. That critical discussion of institutional racism is quite pivotal to the whole project of *Racism, Education and the State*; though the book's focus is largely on the level of education politics, that critique is clearly the conceptual means of linking these discussions to the politics of education, as well the basis of the later critique of the practical shortcomings of policies based on such shifting theoretical sands.

In their chapter on institutional racism Troyna and Williams do in fact set out an agenda for the effective clarification of the concept:

> First, a clear and unambiguous outline of the nature of the relationship between institutions. Second, an understanding of the operation and workings of particular institutions. Third, an appreciation of the relationship between individuals who are part of the institution and the structures within which they work (Troyna and Williams, 1986, pp. 55-6)

What is most striking about that agenda in terms of the relationship between education policy and institutionalised racism is its unambiguously structural approach. It provides a basis for conceptualising that relationship that is not confined to seeing policy as discourse and its outcomes shaped by what the text does or does not say. To be sure, analysing policy as discourse can be important and useful (as Troyna and Williams show in their discussion of institutionalised racism as hidden curriculum), but as their agenda indicates, such analysis by no means provides a comprehensive account of institutional racism nor one that can readily identify its sources or how it might be overcome.

In the rest of this chapter I will try to focus on the relationship between Troyna and Williams' first two points. That is, it seems useful to examine how the relationship between institutions frames and limits the activities of organisations such as schools. This assumes both (i) that the 'opportunity' for organisations to institutionalise racist practices is not randomly distributed, or a matter of pure contingency, but results from the wider structure of social institutions within which individual institutions are embedded, and (ii) that as a result, the nature and level of practices that are racist in their consequences are not spontaneously generated in the organisations themselves, and cannot be explained on the basis of investigations of individual organisations like schools, or even social institutions like education, in isolation. This approach relies on and reinforces the necessity of comparative analysis in understanding any particular social institution. It draws fundamentally on two major bodies of literature, the 'societal effect' (see Maurice *et al*, 1986) and the 'new institutionalism' (see Powell and DiMaggio, 1993).

Work on the societal effect demonstrates how social institutions combine 'organically in nationally distinct ways; social institutions such as law, education, political institutions take their shape from the ways they interact with and influence each other.

The idea of the societal effect was developed by researchers investigating the sources of different patterns of work organisation in different societies. In a nutshell what they concluded was that none of the practices they were comparing could be explained in isolation. The whole ensemble of social institutions that surrounded the organisation of work – legal, financial, industrial relations, vocational education, division of labour – constituted an organic and nationally specific and unique whole. To understand any part of that whole it was necessary to understand how it related to the other component institutions.

The new institutionalism complements this approach by insisting that institutions and organisations take on the forms they do through their unique responses being to the challenges they face, with the main resource for those responses being the institution or organisation's existing procedures. The institution or organisation's mode of operation and their interpretation of and adjustment to significant changes in the context of their operation are based on conceptions of what is appropriate within the existing organisation framework, rather than designed to maximise some objective notion of efficiency or effectiveness.

The discussion will consider very briefly three aspects of how the structures of policy making themselves create 'opportunities' for institutionalised racism to take root in an organisation: the political structures through which 'race-related' policies are made; the relationship of a range of social institutions and institutionalised racism; and the contribution of the modes of operation of those institutions.

Policy making structures

The forms and processes taken by institutionalised racism inevitably reflect the formal channels through which official, formal, overt, race related policies are made. It is in this area that implicit ethnocentric assumptions are perhaps most likely to be made. The Treaty of Waitangi, Brown *vs.* the Board of Education and LEAs mean little if anything outside their countries of origin but they account for major differences not only in the race related policies of New Zealand, the United States and England respectively , but also for the differences between those countries in the opportunities for, and direction of, institutionalised racism.

The first refers to a treaty based settlement between colonising and colonised peoples that was to form the basis of their shared occupation of the same national territory; 'the principles of the Treaty of Waitangi' are still daily invoked and remain basic to (though they by no means exhaust) considerations of 'race relations' in New Zealand education. They are all the more important since New Zealand is a unitary state with a national education policy. The (uni-cameral) Parliament is sovereign; there are no strong institutions of civil society, such as churches, trade unions or regional groupings that could provide countervailing power to that of the state, and there are few, if any, legal constraints on the power of the government. This means that central government is the dominant factor in policy formation and in the oversight of its (devolved) implementation, the major constraint in race related matters is the requirement to honour the principles of the Treaty. Here, racism would be institutionalised through the ability to install local interpretations of national policy and through the flexibility of the Treaty principles themselves.

In the United States, by contrast, race related policy has been much more a matter for Federal and State legal jurisdictions whose concern has been above all to guarantee equal rights to all individuals. Education policy has been shaped most fundamentally by these legally rather than politically or educationally initiated moves. Here, racism would be institutionalised through the nature of the legal framework and through its interstices, interpretations and loopholes.

Finally, the English case shows how changing policies change the contexts in which 'unofficial' racism can become institutionalised. In the 1980's, as Troyna and Williams (1986) show so clearly, the absence of any policy lead from central government enabled some Local Education Authorities (who in any case at that time enjoyed a high level of formal autonomy in education policy), to promote their own antiracist initiatives. However, these very initiatives were to become important grounds for the Thatcher government to curtail drastically the powers of LEAs. They were replaced by policies almost entirely deracialised at a formal level (in itself, of course, a way of central government exercising its agenda setting power). This absence of formal policy; part of a much wider shift to a smaller, stronger state that saw government withdraw from responsibility for many if not all the public good features of education; left the way open for the development of two kinds of institutionalised racism. One was based on the increasingly prominent discursive emphasis on the nature and importance of 'Englishness'. This found its way into formal education policy through discussions on the content of the National Curriculum, especially in History. Informally, it created new criteria of national belongingness and identity that inevitably impacted on both the nature and degree of institutionalised racism in education and elsewhere. The second reflected the government's withdrawal from responsibility for social policy. It was based on the replacement of the notion of equality by that of equity, confining equality to equality before the law, and of the notion of entitlement by that of fair competition in the market place.

These moves, which had their equivalents in New Zealand and the US, opened up the governance of education policy and practice to a far wider range of social institutions than heretofore. It is to the consequences of this shift that we now turn.

Social institutions and institutionalised racism

Discussions of institutionalised racism frequently seem to assume that it is intrinsically a state-related phenomenon. Further, they often confine themselves to how it is brought about by, or encouraged or enabled by, state regulation (whether national or local) and bureaucratic practice. Here I want to demonstrate the shortcomings and dangers of that assumption by focusing on the effects on the governance of education of the changes that have been brought about in most Western countries and in the way that the co-ordination of social policy is brought about. (This discussion is a highly condensed version of arguments developed in Dale, 1996 and 1997). No longer is that coordination solely the preserve of the state operating through a democratic form (though arguably it remains ultimately the state's responsibility). One consequence of the widespread move to the 'smaller, stronger state' has been that over a wide (though intentionally varying) area, the state, instead of carrying out a range of social policies through its own agencies, now restricts itself to determining — and possibly monitoring — which non state (or quasi state) agencies shall take over its co-ordinating role. The most prominent examples are probably the devolution of the management of schools to local 'communities' and the alleged shift to a market form of provision of schooling. More systematically, we may see three major institutions of social co-ordination, the state, the market and the 'community' becoming involved in the governance of schooling; while the process of governance itself can be broken down into funding, provision (or delivery) and regulation functions. This gives us formally a 3 x 3 table with potentially any one of the functions to be carried out by any one (or more) of the institutions (though for the state to retain a minimum level of control over the education system it would need to retain control over regulation — but not funding or provision). The implications of these shifts for institutionalised racism are complex. Essentially they entail a multiplication of the ways that racism can be institutionalised in education, though not necessarily, of course, an overall increase in the prevalence of the phenomenon. Indeed, it might be inferred from the traditional emphasis on the central role of the state in bringing about institutional racism that its relatively lower profile in the funding, provision and regulation of education might enable some forms of the phenomenon to be eliminated. Moving control of schools closer to those they actually serve is presented as allowing them to make decisions that best suit their own circumstances. On the other hand, it might be seen as providing opportunities for local racists to have more influence through gaining control of school management bodies. Similarly, its proponents assert that the market is the fairest means of the distribution of all goods and services because it is totally non discriminatory; its fundamental commitment to the idea that anybody's money is as good as anyone else's means that it is colour blind and gender blind and that consequently there is no basis on which racist or sexist practices could be institutionalised. Sadly, the evidence from the labour market and the housing market suggests that early examples of racial discrimination in the burgeoning education market are unlikely to be isolated or untypical. Nevertheless, these changes open up new and very important sites for the investigation of the forms, causes and consequences of institutionalised racism.

Modes of institutional operation

The formal 3x3 table of the governance of education does not tell the whole story. This is clear if we consider for a moment the claim that education has been 'privatised' in this process of governmental withdrawal. In terms of the table this would mean that market institutions had taken over from the state the provision, and possibly the funding and regulation of education. Of course, this has not happened anywhere (with the possible exception of Chile). What has occurred has been a shift within the state from a bureaucratic mode of operation to a market-like mode of operation. The clearest example of this is the way that access to schools is no longer entirely determined by bureaucratic procedures that apply universally, but by schools being placed by legislation in a competitive relationship with each other that determines how they will seek to improve the quality and/or the quantity of their student body. For instance, schools, rather than becoming market institutions are being required to operate in a market mode. Not only, then, has the state divested itself of certain functions, it has also taken on new modes of operation and is no longer confined to the bureaucratic universalist mode.

Here again, the consequences for the forms and frequency of institutionalised racism are complex; they could either reinforce or weaken it. However, we should note that not all parts of institutions nor all their operations are necessarily equally affected by changes in the mode of operation. Changes in schools' recruitment policies and practices, for instance, may or may not entail similar changes in, say, their streaming policies and practices. Of particular importance here is what may be the most intractable mode of operation in schools, the traditional professional mode, which basically states that the teacher's job is to treat all children alike as individuals. This combination of universalism and individualism has often been identified as a contributory factor in the institutionalisation of racism and it is not at all clear what effect the changes in the governance of education might have on it.

Conclusion

This very brief consideration of how the 'opportunity structure' for institutionalised racism might be generated and shaped is necessarily somewhat inconclusive. Nevertheless, it seems important to examine the phenomenon at this level. Comparative analysis shows how structures of opportunity for institutionalised racism to be installed themselves vary. Thus suggests another level at which both analysis and preventative action might be carried out. Barry Troyna's later work was clearly most sympathetic to this approach (cf Halpin and Troyna 1995) and this small contribution is offered as a minor addition to what we all hope will be a continuously growing body of work stimulated by the fine scholar and friend this volume celebrates.

References

Clifford, J. and Dhareshwar, V. (1989) "Preface' Travelling Theories: Travelling Theorists', *Inscriptions* 5, pp.v-vii

Dale, R. (1994) 'Applied Education Politics or the Political Sociology of Education?' Halpin, D. and Troyna, B. (Eds.) *Researching Education Policy: Ethical and Methodological Issues,* London, Falmer

Dale, R. (1996) 'The Governance of Education', Unpublished Paper, University of Auckland Department of Education

Dale, R. (1997) 'The State and the Governance of Education: An Analysis of the Restructuring of the State-Education Relationship', Halsey, A., Brown, P., Lauder, H. and Stuart Wells, A. (Eds.) *Education: Culture, Economy, Society* Oxford, Oxford University Press, pp. 273-282

Halpin, D. and Troyna, B. (1995) 'The Politics of Education Policy Borrowing', *Comparative Education* 31,3,303-310

Johnston, P. M. (1997) 'Education Policy for Maori: Mechanisms of Power and Difference', Unpublished Ph D thesis, University of Auckland

Maurice, M., Sellier, F. and Silvestre, J-J. (1986) *The Social Foundations of Industrial Power,* Cambridge, MIT Press

Mead, L. T. (1996) 'Nga Aho o te Kakahu Matauranga; the Multiple Layers of Struggle by Maori in Education', Unpublished PhD thesis, University of Auckland

Powell, W. and DiMaggio, P. (Eds.) (1993) *The New Institutionalism in Organizational Analysis,* Chicago, University of Chicago Press

Smith, G. H.(1997) 'The Development of Kaupapa Maori theory and practice', Unpublished PhD thesis, University of Auckland

Troyna, B. and Williams, J. (1986) *Racism, Education and the State,* London, Croom Helm

10

THE STATE AND EDUCATION POLICY: THE CONTRIBUTION OF THE WORK OF BARRY TROYNA[1]

Bob Lingard

Introduction

This chapter outlines Barry Troyna's contribution to our understanding of the state in educational policy production, particularly, but not exclusively, in relation to antiracism policies. The state has had a number of comings and goings in social theory. There has been considerable documentation of the way a concern with the state was washed away in much empirical and theoretical social science work after the second world war and brought back in – 'reinstated' – from the late seventies. There has now been what Emy and James (1996, p.27) call a 'second retreat from the state' under the impact of poststructuralism and the work of Foucault on governmentality which, perhaps paradoxically, in accepting that 'power is everywhere', down plays the significance of state power (Hinkson, 1996, p.198). This new theoretical basis for a retreat from the state as too unitary and unified a concept, sees the state instead 'as always dissolved into multiple and changing sites of micro-power' and as simply 'a contingent collection of contingent processes' (Emy and James, 1996, p.29).

The chapter thus seeks to locate Barry Troyna's work in the context of the first reinstatement of the state in social theory and the second poststructuralist driven retreat from it. Troyna's theoretical position on the state is linked to his stance of 'critical social research' whereby research is not only about understanding the relationships between specific events and underlying social relations but is to be utilised in support of political struggles (Troyna, 1994, p.73). Such a stance is nowhere more obvious than in his extensive work on antiracism policies and practices, especially in relation to local government activism. I am conscious here in that referring to Barry Troyna alone I may be accused of neglecting the fact that much of his work was done with others, which also reflected his political stance.

The Racialised State

The sociology of education in contemporary Britain was reframed by the Tory reconstruction of education in England and Wales, particularly through the 1988 Education Reform Act. This reframing witnessed a new focus on educational policy and the role of the state in all aspects of what Bowe, Ball and Gold (1992) have called the 'policy cycle', stretching from the production of policy texts within the state to their practice in schools. A new genre of what Jenny Ozga has called 'policy sociology', which is 'rooted in the social science tradition, historically informed and drawing on qualitative and illuminative techniques' (1987, p.144), was spawned. Roger Dale's *The State and Education Policy* (1989), which takes an Offean approach to the state in its analysis of the new policy settlement constructed by Thatcherism, and Stephen Ball's (1990) *Politics and Policy Making in Education* (1990), which analysed the education state and the micro-politics within it in the production of the Act, became the benchmarks within this new genre.

At another level both of these important studies were manifestations of the new work on the state which was occurring within the social sciences. Each operated within a different framework. Dale sought to understand the state in terms of the balancing act it had to perform between accumulation and legitimation pressures upon it, while also emphasising the way in which state structures mediated policy pressures of various sorts. Ball wanted to stress the space between economic pressures and politics and, specifically, between the former and educational policy production. He documented the internal state contests and the agency of policy workers involved in policy text production. Both sought to move away from an instrumental and unified conception of the state with Dale's work concerned with the new macro Tory educational policy settlement and Ball focusing on the micro-politics inside the state involved in the production of specific elements of that settlement.

Barry Troyna's work on the state and antiracism policies in Local Education Authorities began well prior to the Education Reform Act and the new policy sociology genre. *Racism, Education and the State: The Racialisation of Education Policy*, co-authored with Jenny Williams, for example, was published in 1986 and while the educational changes wrought by the Tories provided the backdrop to this account, the focus was on Local Education Authorities where 'progressive' policies were still being formulated. Much of this was to change after the passing of the Education Reform Act of 1988. As Troyna and Vincent (1995, p.161) have observed, 'The 1988 Education Reform Act and subsequent legislation seemed to mark the end for the LEAs as creative partners in educational decision and policy-making'. Written in 1986, *Racism, Education and the State* points out the neglect of policy production in educational research up to that time. Troyna and Williams also note that it was only from the early 1980s that LEAs began to formulate specific policies in relation to questions of racism in education, thus providing something on which researchers could focus. However, and importantly, they argue that the failure of these Local Authorities to develop such policies prior to this time did not mean that there were not problems of racism in education. Indeed, in this respect they stress the significance of the surreptitious link between the politics of non-decision making and broader power relations. The lack of antiracist policies tells us as much about power relations and policy as does the situation from the early eighties when LEAs began to formulate such policies. What state actors do *not do* should be important to policy researchers. This is an important insight derived from Troyna's work on the state and policy production.

While acknowledging the tendentious nature of the concept of 'race', Troyna and Williams draw our attention to a 'racialised' state and 'deracialised' and 'racialised' policy discourses in education; important observations which remain hidden in much subsequent state and policy theorising in education. The state is racialised irrespective of whether or not its specific policies are framed by racialised or deracialised discourses, as is policy for that matter. (Troyna has made a similar pertinent point about teachers and teaching.) As Toni Morrison (1992, pp.12-13) noted in *Playing in the Dark: whiteness and the literary imagination*, 'in a wholly racialised society, there is no escape from racially inflected language'. Racialised policy discourses can be progressive but at the same time work to 'other' those considered to be 'raced', that is, non-whites. Troyna and Williams's insight here was an early precursor to subsequent theorising which seeks to deconstruct what Morrison has called the 'textual strategies' which establish 'impenetrable whiteness'. Just as feminism 'gave' men a gender, such theorising recognised all as 'racialised' subjects, and at the same time rejected the assumption that the 'universal subjects' of both history and theory were 'non-racialised' and without gender. In this respect, *Racism, Education and the State* was a forerunner of such post colonial developments.

The focus of *Racism, Education and the State* is upon the shift within some Local Education Authorities from multicultural educational policies of the sixties and seventies to antiracism policies of the eighties, a move from deracialised to racialised approaches. This entails detailed empirical work and a focus upon both policy discourses and the relationship between the local and national state. In terms of policy discourses Troyna and Williams utilise Apple's concept of 'slogan systems' (1979) to analyse the suturing together of disparate views in policy statements which then work to appease various competing interests. Such a perspective rejects the rational account of policy texts and instead emphasises their political character. Troyna and Williams note in relation to antiracism policies:

> Antiracist policies are, then, negotiated products of academic and political debate about the terms racism and institutional racism; the selective incorporation of specific demands made by groups who enjoy differential access to power; and particular professional understandings of the purpose of education and its potential as an agent of social and political change. In blunt terms, policies constitute a negotiated settlement – evidence of the way in which conflicts are resolved formally in bureaucratic and political settings. (Troyna and Williams, 1986, p.99)

In subsequent work on social justice policies in education, Troyna (with Carol Vincent) (1995) pursued further this capacity of policy language to charm (p.149). Troyna had this ongoing interest in the politics of language and the language of politics. Such an insight has been developed in the more recent poststructuralist informed policy sociology of Stephen Ball's (1994a) where he distinguishes and relates policy as text and policy as discourse in an attempt to encapsulate both the constraints and freedom involved in policy practice.

Changes from deracialised to racialised policy discourses are traced in *Racism, Education and the State*, and the significance of academic research on racism and the importance of changing theories of poor school performance by black students as a result of such changes, are clearly documented. However, a broader structural analysis is also provided to explain why the policy discourses of some LEAs have been racialised and others not. Here Troyna and Williams argue that ideological, political and economic developments during the late seventies and eighties saw race become an important element in the politics of some cities; particularly those in industrial decline and with racially segmented labour forces. Education and educational politics were important sites where these racial inequalities were played out. Consequently, Troyna and Williams see LEAs as 'sites of struggle' in respect of these matters which 'determine' particular policy responses. Further, they document a number of 'educational crises' which occurred from the late seventies in respect of black students. The first was the establishment of the Swann inquiry set up by the central government in 1979 to investigate the 'underachievement of black students' which questioned the accuracy of the account of schools as part of the meritocracy. The second was the partial severing of the relationship between the possession of schooling credentials and guaranteed transition to a job for black youth, while the third related to the 'pluralist dilemma in education' (p.116) in respect of how different cultures and knowledges ought to be valued and represented in schools. Some LEAs, under political pressure, thus developed antiracist policies, moving away from the deracialised discourses of multiculturalism.

It is in that context that Troyna and Williams take a contingent view of LEA policy responses. They note:

> The relative autonomy of LEAs, however, creates 'space' for the articulation of policies which might assume one of a number of orientations and emphases. Policies might, for instance, embrace liberal notions of multiculturalism and focus on concepts such as 'the truth' and transcultural rationality. These would lead to the development of a depoliticised curriculum. Alternatively, the 'space' might be filled by a range of more radical antiracist initiatives. Whatever the case it is clear that because LEAs are sites of struggle in which local demography, ethnic mobilisation, established political and professional ideologies and teacher organisations each play a greater or lesser role in the determination of policy options, it is impossible to predict how and in what ways this 'space' will be filled. (Troyna and Williams, p.117)

Troyna and Williams also consider the relationship between the central and local state and how this is important in respect of how much space is open to the local site, as well as how it is utilised. The central state and its actions are also framed by economic restructuring and the reorganisation of global capitalism. This space for the local state was very apparent to national Tory governments as indicated in their successful attempts at weakening LEAs through the Education Reform Act of 1988. Troyna and Williams argue that research on policy making in LEAS (remember they were writing in

1986) needs to focus on 'the broad political, social and economic contexts in which policies are generated' (p.7), including the central state, and upon the ways these are 'mediated and redefined' in 'the process of policy generation' at the local sites (LEAs) by 'educational professionals, bureaucrats and local politicians' (p.7). Despite the fact that this research dealt with LEAs, this conceptualisation seems a most useful one for doing policy analysis, particularly of policy production. In many ways, it does not appear too far removed from Bowe, Ball and Gold's (1992) 'policy cycle' approach which acknowledged the interactive relationships between the contexts of influence, text production and practice within the policy cycle. One difference is the emphasis given to the state in policy text production, but this is also a question of what sort of policies a specific piece of research is focusing upon.

While the Troyna approach to the state is clearly a structuralist one, there is a focus upon its internal differentiation, not unlike the 'dual state theory' of Cawson and Saunders (1983), where the central and local elements of the state are less or more pluralist in orientation and focused less or more on economic policies (accumulation) or social policies (legitimation). Further, there is a move beyond a straightforward instrumental conception of the state in the rejection of a simple, unmediated capital, state, policy, educational policy relationship. There is, of course, still much empirical and theoretical work to do, on the changing relationships between the two arms of the state; Troyna and Williams recognised the constraints placed by the central state on local policy options. In terms of state/civil society connections, Troyna and Williams utilise the work of Ben-Tovim and colleagues to speak of an 'extended' or 'integral' state to include professional associations, trade unions, voluntary associations and so on which can put policy pressure upon the local arm of the state.

Policy Sociology

Troyna entered the policy sociology debate in a 1994 paper, in the edited collection with David Halpin (1994), and more specifically in a paper with Richard Hatcher (1994) in which they critiqued the concept of 'policy cycle', a concept developed by Stephen Ball in his second policy sociology text written with Richard Bowe and Anne Gold (1992) entitled *Reforming Education and Changing Schools.* While Ball's (1990) *Politics and Policy Making in Education* focused on the production of policy by the state, the second study considered the way such policy was taken up in schools, thus the title of the book. Here policy is considered as both text and process and in rejecting a linear top-down educational administration account of policy production 'followed' temporally and in intent by implementation, the concept of a policy cycle consisting of three interactive contexts was developed. In creating this approach Bowe, Ball and Gold criticised the policy sociology of Roger Dale, characterising his work as state-centric and as a more sophisticated version of the top-down, linear conception of the relationship between policy production and implementation. In a sense, this debate has been clouded by a failure to consider which approach is appropriate to a particular empirical focus for policy research. For example, research on state policy production would surely grant greater emphasis to state structures and internal politics than would research looking at the practice of a specific state policy in a school. Further, it is often the case that schools under local contexts of influence do develop policies of their own prior to the development and mandating of such policies by the state.

Hatcher and Troyna's debate with Ball is basically one concerning the nature of relationships between broad economic and social relations, the state and politics, and state policy and (in education) its practice in schools, a debate about determination versus relative autonomy. This debate is also framed by differing structuralist and poststructuralist conceptions of power. Structuralists tend to see power as possessed, centred and done to others as a form of coercion, while poststructuralists, drawing on Foucault, tend to see power as relational, dispersed and enabling. Hatcher and Troyna

(1994, p.168) suggest that with the latter 'power is a spider's web without the spider'. This debate then is about the nature of the relationship between the spider and its web or about putting a particular representation of the spider back into the web.

This debate regarding the state and power is just one symptom of a broader debate between structuralist materialist approaches and those which recognise the gains made by poststructuralist theory and the so-called linguistic turn within the social sciences. Hatcher and Troyna and Ball focus upon the state from these different directions: the former want to acknowledge the micropolitics entailed in policy production and practice while holding onto a more deterministic conception of state power and its relationship to wider social and economic power, while the latter wants to acknowledge the limits of state power and the more substantially mediated relationships between capitalist economic power, the state and the politics played out there and the practice of educational policy. Thus in relation to the policy cycle Hatcher and Troyna, in Ball's (1994b, p.180) words, suggest that such an approach accepts that the 'forcefulness of policy is always subordinate to the interpretational responses of situated social actors'. Ball rejects this as an account of what he is attempting to depict and theorise. Again, there is the neglected question here of what is the focus of a particular piece of research and what is it we are attempting to theorise. There is a way in which both – perhaps without recognising it – want to acknowledge the impact of restructured global capitalism, its relationships to a specific state and its politics, and still allow for micropolitics and agency. (Ball (1994b) is perhaps suggesting more than what is usually understood by 'agency' in relation to teachers and policy in his talk of the 'chaos/freedom of the ordinary' (p.177) which exists beyond the binary of domination and resistance.) Hatcher and Troyna and Ball come at this 'problem' from different directions: Troyna's work on the racialised state emphasised the state's non-instrumental and non-unitary character, while all of his work has been at pains to reject a class reductionism and also recognise the salience of race, and to a much lesser extent, gender, while Stephen Ball, *pace* Dale (1992), also acknowledges that the state is one necessary but not sufficient focus of policy sociology. However, in their emphases on the empiricism of the specific there is some commonality in their work.

The Hatcher and Troyna debate with Ball around the policy cycle is really a debate between neo- and post-structuralism. There is a sense in which they are both working on *the* problem within contemporary social theory as inflected by poststructuralist insights and the continuing need to recognise structures and material effects without constituting a new grand theory, which is 'closed and certain' (Ball, 1994b).

There is a way in which some recent post-poststructuralist work seeks to do this (Hindess, 1996) with its recognition of both enabling and constraining conceptions of power and the role of the state and non-state. In my view a new position derived from the meeting of neo- and post- structuralism is required to theorise the state and policy cycle. As Hinkson (1996, p.198) has recently argued: 'A dualism between 'totalising' forms, which correspond to grand narratives, and post-modern specificity and decentredness apparently leaves little conceptual space for a post-modern state'. The Hatcher and Troyna debate with Stephen Ball has contributed towards the emergence of such an approach – a theory of the post-modern state. This is not however, only a theoretical debate, but rather one also located in those economic, political and cultural changes which the concepts of 'globalisation' and 'postmodernity' attempt to encapsulate in short-hand ways. Whether one accepts a 'besieged' or 'defiant ' perspective of the nation state (Reus-Smit, 1996) in relation to these pressures, our theory must seek to understand them so as to contribute to effective political strategies.

The political character and commitment of Barry Troyna's academic work has been noted. In relation to *Racism, Education and the State*, he observes: Jenny Williams and I were also determined that our research should feed into the political struggles waged by black and antiracist campaigners both in national and local arenas' (Troyna, 1994, p.73). It is this position which also makes him critical of policy sociology, noting that, while it has much in common with critical social science research, 'What it does not do is harness that analysis to an explicit political commitment to change things' (Troyna, 1994, p.72). Troyna is also critical of the nomenclature of 'policy sociology', arguing instead that critical social science would be a better classification, given its inter- and cross-disciplinary character. Furthermore, he argues that this research and theorising ought to take more account of feminist and antiracist work (Troyna, 1994, p.81).

Conclusion

This chapter has argued that Barry Troyna's work on the state and education policy has made a number of significant contributions, not the least of which was its early recognition of the need for such educational policy research. Because of his work we are better aware of: the racialised character of the state and its policy discourses; the need to analyse policy inaction and silences as well as policy action and statements; the need to consider policy as discourse and the political work it does in suturing together different interests; the differentiated character of the interior of the state and the need to research the relationships between local and national arms of it; the need to move beyond a class reductionism when considering state relations with civil society and when considering the internal micropolitics of the state itself; the necessity of identifying, through research and theorising, strategies for change. And finally, in the debate between neo- and post- structuralist accounts of the state and the policy cycle we have seen the ground cleared for an emerging theory of the post-modern state in a globalised, diasporic, post-colonial (in aspirations at least) world – yet another 'reinstatement' of the state in contemporary social theory post the poststructuralist retreat from it.

References

Apple, M. (1979) *Ideology and Curriculum*, London, Routledge and Kegan Paul

Ball, S.J. (1994a) *Education Reform: A Critical and Post-Structural Approach*, Buckingham, Open University Press

Ball, S.J. (1994b) 'Some Reflections on Policy Theory: A Brief Response to Hatcher and Troyna', *Journal of Education Policy*, 8, 2, pp.171-182

Ball, S.J. (1990) *Politics and Policy Making in Education*, London, Routledge

Bowe, R., Ball, S. and Gold, A. (1992) *Reforming Education and Changing Schools*, London, Routledge

Cawson, A. and Saunders, P. (1983) 'Corporatism, Competitive Politics and Class Struggle' in King, R.(Ed.) *Capital Politics*, London, Routledge and Kegan Paul, pp.8-28

Dale, R. (1989) *The State and Education Policy*, Milton Keynes, Open University Press

Dale, R. (1992) 'Review Essay: Whither the State and Education Policy? recent work in Australia and New Zealand', *British Journal of Sociology of Education*, 13, 3, pp.387-395

Emy, H. and James, P. (1996) 'Debating the State: The Real Reasons for Bringing the State Back in' James, P. (Ed.) *The State in Question: Transformations of the Australian State*, Sydney, Allen and Unwin, pp.8-37

Halpin, D. and Troyna, B. (Eds.) (1994) *Researching Education Policy: Ethical and Methodological Issues*, London, Falmer

Hatcher, R. and Troyna, B. (1994) 'The 'Policy Cycle': a Ball by Ball account', *Journal of Education Policy*, 9, 2, pp.155-170

Hindess, B. (1996) *Discourses of Power: from Hobbes to Foucault*, Oxford, Blackwell

Hinkson, J. (1996) 'The State of Postmodernity: Beyond Cultural Nostalgia Or Pessimism in James, P. (Ed.) *The State in Question: Transformations of the Australian State*, Sydney, Allen and Unwin, pp. 196-223

Morrison, T. (1992) *Playing in the Dark: Whiteness and the Literary Imagination*, Cambridge, Massachusetts, Harvard University Press

Ozga, J. (1987) 'Studying Education Through the Lives of Policy-makers' in Barton, L. and Walker, S. (Eds.) *Changing Policies, Changing Teachers*, Milton Keynes, Open University Press, p.138-150

Reus-Smit, C. (1996) 'Beyond Foreign Policy: State Theory and the Changing Global Order' in James, P.(Ed.) *The State in Question: Transformations of the Australian State*, Sydney, Allen and Unwin, pp. 161-195

Troyna, B. (1994) 'Critical Social Research and Education Policy', *British Journal of Educational Studies*, xxxxii, 1, pp.70-84

Troyna, B. and Vincent, C. (1995) 'The Discourses of Social Justice in Education', *Discourse*, 16, 2, pp.149-166

Troyna, B. and Williams, J. (1986) *Racism, Education and the State: The Racialisation of Education Policy*, London, Croom Helm

Note

1. I would like to thank Sandra Taylor and Miriam Henry for comments on an earlier draft of this chapter.

11

MULTICULTURALISM AND ANTIRACISM RECONSIDERED

John Rex

The term 'multiculturalism' came into general use in reference to political, social, and educational policy in the nineteen eighties. For some it was seen as one aspect of a democratic insistence on equality, but, for others, it was an alternative to equality; those who were marked by differences of appearance or culture were to be singled out for different and, in all probability, unequal, treatment. In schools, in accordance with this second view, the concentration was to be on the exotica of immigrant minority cultures with little attempt being made to ensure equality for minority children. Those who saw that educational policies based on this conception could lead to inequality or at best to paternalism therefore found it necessary to insist on policies to promote equality for these children. With physically visible minorities in mind they described such policies as 'antiracist'.

Amongst social scientists no-one was more insistent on this than my friend and colleague, Barry Troyna. For him multiculturalism was largely a rhetoric of paternalism and inequality and it was therefore necessary to replace the policy of multiculturalism in education with one based on antiracism. His work and that of his colleagues at Warwick therefore played an important role in setting up what came to be understood as the radical position in relation to problems of race and ethnicity in education.

In this article I want to pay tribute to the role which Barry Troyna played in this matter, yet at the same time I want to argue that it may have led to a down-playing by his colleagues of the importance of multiculturalism of a more positive kind in politics, in social policy and in education.

The Democratic and Egalitarian Version of Multicultural Theory

In my own writing (Rex 1996) I have taken as a charter for this more positive view of multiculturalism the well-known definition of 'integration' offered by the Home Secretary, Roy Jenkins, which envisaged in his words, 'not a flattening process of uniformity, but cultural diversity, coupled with equal opportunity, in an atmosphere of mutual tolerance'. I have argued that this makes sense only in terms of the recognition of what I called two 'cultural domains. On the one hand it suggested a shared and unquestionable public political culture based upon equality of opportunity; on the other it allowed for the continuance in the private and communal domain of a variety of cultures based upon a diversity of languages, religions and family practices in minority communities.

In arguing for this kind of multiculturalism in Britain and in Europe I have come to recognise the theoretical and practical problems which it involves. Most sociological theory of the functionalist sort finds it difficult to see the two 'cultural domains' as totally indepen-dent. It regards society and culture as consisting of a set of institu-tions which are mutually supportive of each other. On the other hand, even if it is agreed that the two domains can be independent of each other, it is not clear in which domain different institutions belong. Not least schools are institutions which *prima facie* straddle the two domains.

Dealing first with the theoretical problem one should notice that there are alternatives to the crude form of functionalism, to which I have referred. One is the theory of secularisation which suggests that in modern society the institutions of the polity and the economy have been liberated from simple normative control and operate in accordance with the logic of the market and bureaucracy. A second is the more sophisticated functionalism of Talcott Parsons (Parsons 1951) which, while recognising the importance in modern social systems of the norms of the 'Adaptive' sub-system (the economy), the 'Goal Attainment' sub-system (the polity), and the 'Integrative' sub-system (Law), also adds a fourth sub-system referred to as that of 'Latency' or 'Pattern-Maintenance and Tension Management'. The role of this fourth sub-system is to enable individual actors to withdraw from major activities and, as it were, recharge their batteries. In this theoretical approach the family and the community prepares individual actors psychologically for participation in the larger secular orders, not simply by inculcating the values of those orders but by saving them from a state of anomie. Without the family and the community they would not be capable of functioning as social actors at all.

Theories of social class and citizenship are also relevant here. Marxist and other socialists had usually taken the view that it was the solidarity of social class which resisted the amorality of the secular orders. T.H. Marshall (1950) took this further by arguing that as the working class gained first legal then political and, finally, social rights, a new kind of solidarity, namely that based on citizenship would come to replace that based on class, and, with the winning of social rights, all individuals would be guaranteed equality of opportunity, and, up to a minimum, equality of outcome.

There do in fact seem to be several ways in which some sort of morality or normative order can be thought of as operating in a modern society. The individual actors may be thought of as being psychologically equipped to act through their participation in solitary communities; they may be seen as developing their solidarity in defending themselves against oppression and exploitation in secular society, or they may be seen as imposing a moral order on secular society. It is in these terms that, I think, the struggle for equality comes to form the basis of what I have called the 'shared political culture of the public domain'.

Most of the problems involved here had been worked out in the political theory of ethnically homogenous societies. In the liberal view, a liberal society required the recognition of individual rights; in a more socialist or social democratic view groups with conflicting interests worked out compromises in the institutions of the welfare state. What they did not allow for, however, were minority groups distinguishable from the majority by their appearance or their culture. What the egalitarian or democratic theory of multiculturalism seeks to do therefore is to define the ways in which these minorities can be guaranteed their rights in democratic welfare states.

Schools have an essential but very complex role to play in this process. Clearly they must, together with the family and the local community, offer a basic security to individuals; they must equip them with general and specialised competences to compete for jobs in the market place and in a bureaucratically organised polity; and, in a democratic and egalitarian society, they must inculcate a belief in some measure of equality, a value which may be displaced in societies which are less egalitarian by the notion of freedom of choice.

All of these problems have to be faced in ethnically homogenous societies, but they occur in a new form for immigrant minorities and their children. Such minorities already have their own institutions developed for preparing their children to participate in different types of society. The question now is how these institutions will operate and how they will be seen in a new society of settlement.

The task of initial socialisation will be shared by the community and the primary school. Although it will also have to begin the task of transmitting necessary competences (what we call in English the three r's), these schools will also be engaged in the even more fundamental task of turning the individual into a secure social being. This is important in its own right but may also be the precondition of any other form of learning. Since, however, this task has already been begun in the family and the community, the primary school will have to relate its own agenda of socialisation to those of families and communities. It is in this way that the primary syllabus has to be, in some degree, multicultural.

Minority languages and religions present problems both at the primary and secondary level. So far as language is concerned the main aim of the school in any European society has to be the acquisition by all children of the majority language in that society. Without the ability to use this language there can be no question of the children concerned attaining equality. Insofar as children enter the system at any level without a command of the majority language, however, it may well be the case that it may be necessary for minority language to be used initially as a medium of instruction. The purpose of using minority languages in this way would not be to stand in the way of children learning the majority language, but of making them secure in the learning process so that they can go on to learn the majority language as well as other skills as quickly as possible. Beyond this initial point the fostering of minority languages as distinct from using them as a medium of instruction would have a different rationale. Learning them might well be justified as a means through which the school contributes to the life of the minority community, but this is perhaps less important than giving them the same recognition as is accorded to any foreign language. In England this would mean the teaching of Punjabi, Urdu or Bengali along with French, German and Spanish.

Britain faces particular problems so far as religion is concerned. Unlike some other countries Britain does not exclude religion from its schools. It allows for religious assemblies and for religious instruction yet at the same time has come to allow for different versions of Christian as well as Jewish religion. Here, therefore the question has arisen as to how the immigrant religions of Hinduism, Sikhism and Islam are to be accommodated.

Religious assemblies have sometimes involved Christian worship, but have sometimes simply focussed on some moral theme. Children from minority Christian, non-Christian and non-religious back-grounds have, however been allowed to opt out. This has not satis-fied some conservative critics who demand that assemblies should be religious and that they should be predominantly Christian. Repre-sentatives of new minority communities and religions have therefore demanded that they should be allowed to make alternative provision for their own children. The alternative of basing assemblies on a variety of faiths has gained little support and has, particularly, been strongly opposed by parents who regard themselves as Christian and/or British.

It is in fact a rather strange idea of some multiculturalists that children should learn forms of worship which are an amalgam of various faiths and it is hardly surprising that they have met with resistance. Perhaps the only acceptable argument in their favour is that they enable White British and/or Christian students to gain some knowledge of non-Christian faiths. These arguments are even more important in relation to religious education as a subject removed from the question of collective worship. Here many Religious Education teachers have developed syllabuses to allow children to learn about a variety of faiths without being called upon to adhere to them. Such syllabuses have undoubtedly helped to encourage tolerance, but, like religious assemblies, they have been criticised by a conservative lobby which argues that Religious Education should be 'predominantly Christian'.

Beyond the questions of language and religion there is the wider question of how minority cultures should be handled. Since education in these matters is not protected, as religion is, by having a part in the compulsory syllabus, the questions here have been whether all children should learn about a variety of cultures and whether there should be special courses in their own cultures for minority children. The first of these alternatives has rarely been attempted and, so far as courses for minority children are concerned, they have not been compulsory and have no value in terms of gaining examination credit.

There are in fact strong arguments for keeping any special courses on multiculturalism outside the school syllabus altogether and leaving them to extra-school provision by the minority communities themselves. Outside the school they may well be handled more sensitively than they are likely to be by ill-equipped general teachers.

More important, however, is the question of the general culture which is implicit in the syllabus as a whole. In an imperial society this culture has often reflected imperialist and colonialist ideology. There is therefore a strong case for the development of syllabuses particularly in the arts and humanities which reflect the world of the twentieth century. To give one example it should no longer be possible to teach Indian history simply through an account of the achievements of Clive and Hastings. Much valuable work has therefore been done on syllabus revision in recent years and education in the arts and humanities at least has changed to some extent in the direction of a less Anglo-Centric, Eurocentric direction. Such a change undoubtedly contributes to creating a shared culture which is appropriate to a population containing immigrant ethnic minorities.

A final point which has to be made is that nothing which is proposed in the way of multicultural initiatives should detract from the acquisition of those skills and competences which are necessary for survival in a secular modern world. This is why, Maureen Stone (1980), for example, has argued that even supplementary schooling should concentrate on education in the 'three r's' rather than on fostering minority cultures in order to improve the self-concepts of minority children.

With this said it must be added that there must be a place in the curriculum for political education separate from other subjects which fosters the idea of a society based upon equality for both working-class or disadvantaged British children and for children from minority backgrounds. Of course there will be a fear that such political education will be used for politically partisan purposes or for imposing political dogmas, but there is no reason why syllabuses should not be worked out which guarantee open-mindedness and objectivity about these questions.

Antiracism in Schools

It should be clear from what I have said thus far that multi-culturalism is not an alternative to antiracism in education if it is understood in its democratic and egalitarian form. Nor can anti-racism be seen as divorced from multiculturalism. A sensible multi-cultural programme of the type which I have outlined can contribute both to tolerance towards minorities and perhaps towards a shared political culture appropriate to the twentieth century and beyond. It is itself inherently 'antiracist' and has in fact been increasingly supported by teachers, who, under the influence of guidance from local authorities, are less likely than they once were to reflect the racial and Anglo-centric prejudices of their society.

To say this, however, is not to say that racist attitudes, racial discrimination and downright racial hostility are not to be found amongst teachers and British students. So long as this is the case racism has to be seen as a disciplinary offence. This need not, and should not involve some sort of mechanical form of 'political correctness' which, if it is practised, invites ridicule and is counter-productive. What it has to address itself to is the creation of an environment in which minority children have real equality of oppor-tunity and are not prevented from having it by racial and ethnic discrimination, racial abuse and racial attack.

One further possibility is that of requiring teachers to take courses in 'racial awareness' in order that they should become aware of and self-critical about their own unconscious beliefs and attitudes. This may have some merit if the teachers concerned see the need for such self-criticism. If they do not see such a need and are forced or offered inducements to take such courses, however, they may have the same consequences as mechanical attempts to produce political correctness.

The task facing democrats in British school, it seems to me, is that of creating a consensus in favour of a fair and equal society. Multicultural and antiracist policies taken together in a sensitive way can achieve this. There are, however, many dangers along the way and insensitive attempts to introduce either multiculturalism or anti-racism may easily produce opposite effects to those intended. The best legacy of the work of Barry Troyna would be the creation of a school culture in which sensible and moderate forms of multi-culturalism underpin the creation of antiracist schools and an anti-racist society.

References

Marshall, T.H. (1950) *Citizenship and Social Class,* Cambridge, Cambridge University Press

Parsons, T., (1951) *The Social System,* London, Tavistock

Rex, J., (1996) *Ethnic Minorities in the Modern Nation State,* Basingstoke, Macmillan

Stone, M. (1980) *The Education of the Black Child in Britain – The Myth of Multiracial Education,* London, Collins Fontana

12

SOCIAL JUSTICE IN EDUCATION AFTER THE CONSERVATIVES: THE RELEVANCE OF BARRY TROYNA'S WORK

Richard Hatcher

Perhaps the most effective way we can pay tribute to Barry Troyna is to continue to make creative use of his ideas. Although in the last few years Troyna developed his interests in methodological issues and in the wider education policy debate, he is best known for the critique of multicultural education, and the defence of a particular conception of antiracist education, which was the principal theme of his writings in the 1980s and which he continued to maintain in the 1990s. Now, as a new period in education opens up with the election of a Labour government, it is worth reminding ourselves of the specific context in which many of the most important developments in multicultural and antiracist education took place: that of local education authorities, almost all of which were controlled by the Labour Party. Multicultural education was one of the key elements, both ideologically and in practice, of an agenda of social-democratic reformism within local government which flourished and then declined in the period from the late 1970s to the mid-1980s. Barry Troyna's writings on it represent a sustained critique of that Labourist agenda which has a particular relevance to the Labour government's education policy today.

In *Racism and Education* (1993) Troyna refers to Roger Dale's (1986) distinction between three approaches to the study of policymaking in education. The social administration project was concerned with potential policy problems. The policy analysis project was concerned with the relationship between policy aims and delivery. The social science project was concerned with 'finding out how things are and how they came to be that way' (p.22). This was the approach that Troyna identified himself with. His view was that

> It is imperative, then, that we deconstruct the versions of reality enshrined in policies and explicate the values which underpin and guide them. In this way we are able to identify precisely whose versions of an 'ideal society' they represent. (1993: p.37)

As Rizvi says in his introduction to *Racism and Education*, 'Unlike the traditional approach to policy analysis which takes existing institutions and social and power relations for granted, Troyna's approach makes them problematic' (Rizvi, 1993: p.5). This is an approach which can be applied fruitfully to the new post-Conservative reform agendas, and in particular to those of the Labour Party itself and of the discourse of school effectiveness and school improvement on which Labour policy bases itself.

My purpose here is not to attempt a rounded analysis, but to draw out some of the themes of Troyna's critique of multicultural education in the 1980s which seem to me to have significant relevance for understanding post-Conservative education in the 1990s. I will focus on racial equality, but I will also suggest some parallels with issues of social class and gender inequality in education.

Racial forms of education

One of Troyna's principal concerns was how 'race' was constructed in educational discourse. He made frequent use of Frank Reeves' (1983) terminology, and also Miles' (1988), of *racialisation and deracialisation*, with racist and 'benign' forms of each. He saw the racial forms of education of the 1960s and 1970s as exemplars of a deracialised discourse. 'By obscuring the realities of racism in the education system, both monocultural and multicultural education helped to sustain the ideological facade of equality of opportunity'

(Troyna, 1993: p.30). During the 1980s a number of Labour LEAs developed new discourses of racial equality, which Troyna analysed in his case-studies of the Inner London Education Authority and Manchester LEA. His evaluation of them was critical:

> The radical departure of racialised policies from deracialised understandings of the relationship between black pupils and the education system is more apparent than real. [...] The conception of antiracist education which they embraced tended to retain and reproduce many of the theoretical weaknesses and ideological perspectives more commonly associated with multicultural education. (1993: p.41)

The gains, albeit limited, represented by 'municipal antiracism' in education, were soon to be put into question. The government's 1988 Education Act signalled the return to a deracialised discourse of assimilation. Troyna quoted Sally Tomlinson's observation that

> despite the presence in the education system of over half a million children and young people perceived as racially or ethnically different to a white norm, there was no mention in the Act of race, ethnicity or even multicultural education. (quoted in Troyna and Carrington, 1990: 96)

New Labour, education and racial equality

In May 1997 the long period of Conservative government came to an end with the election of a Labour government led by Tony Blair. This was the Labour Party reinvented as 'New Labour' to distinguish and distance itself from what was seen as 'old Labour', typified by the left-wing Labour councils of the 1980s. The question now is, to which of Troyna's categories of 'race and education' – the deracialised assimilationism of the 1970s, the multiculturalism exemplified by the Swann Report (DES, 1985), the antiracist education of certain local authorities in the 1980s, the return to assimilationism signalled by the 1988 Act – does education policy under New Labour correspond most closely?

Troyna began to answer this question in '*British Schools for British Citizens*'? (Troyna and Hatcher, 1991), which commented on three Labour Party education policy papers published in 1989. We noted that *Multicultural Education: Labour's policy for schools* (Labour Party, 1989a) exemplified the multiculturalism associated with the Swann report. More revealing was what happened to the issue of racial equality in Labour's perspective for education as a whole, elaborated in the Policy Review document *Good Education for All* (Labour Party, 1989b). We said that

> The overwhelmingly dominant theme of the document is education's economic role, to which its social role is subordinate and ancillary. [...] The consequence is that racial equality achieves only a token reference. Racial inequality is subsumed into the general argument that higher standards can be achieved if schools are 'effective'. There is no mention of antiracist teaching. It is as if the experiences of the last ten years of antiracist education had never happened. (Troyna and Hatcher, 1991: p.294)

The token and marginal status of the issue of racial equality, subsumed into the 'effective schools' theme, was confirmed by the third and much more detailed document *Children First* (Labour Party, 1989c), which made no mention of 'race', or indeed gender or class, in its 42 pages.

Troyna's initial assessment of Labour's discourse in the 1990s as deracialised and assimilationist is borne out by an examination of the most recent and authoritative of Labour Party education policy documents. This is what *Opening doors to a learning society* (Labour Party, 1994), a 31 page policy statement, says about racial equality:

> At the moment there is an unacceptable spread of attainment and underachievement in different cultures. All individuals should be respected and treated equally; different cultures must be treated with respect and given freedom of expression. Racial discrimination and religious prejudice have no place in a

modern education system. Local authorities should draw up a statement of aims on multicultural education.' (p12)

This statement is followed by the claim that 'As a nation we cannot afford the social and economic consequences of inequality', and exhortations to listen to the voices of ethnic minority parents and tackle racial harassment. If this were a statement of intent which was followed up with specific measures to implement it, as an integral part of the rest of Labour's education policies, it would mark a return to at least the rhetoric of those Labour LEAs Troyna studied in the 1980s. But it isn't. For example, in the same document, the section on 'effective learning' makes no mention of the implications of 'race' for the curriculum, and criticises Conservative cuts in Section 11 funding while making no commitment to reverse them. *Opening doors to a learning society* was followed a year later by *Excellence for everyone* (Labour Party, 1995), subtitled *Labour's crusade to raise standards*. Since differences in attainment by different ethnic groups have been a key concern for twenty years, and the subject of two major reports (Rampton and Swann), it is all the more remarkable that in this 38 page document there is (apart from a passing reference to black mentoring) no mention of this issue at all. Even the section on exclusions makes no reference to the over-representation of black pupils, a fact now well-established (see Gillborn and Gipps, 1996; Sewell, 1997). It is a totally deracialised discourse.

The contrast between Labour's perspective today and the earlier, multicultural, phase of Labour policy is striking. Then, the key to problems of achievement among ethnic minority pupils was seen to lie in reforming the curriculum to bridge the cultural gap. Its weakness was its all too often superficial notion of ethnic cultures and its reluctance to explicitly address racism. Now, ethnic differences in achievement are assimilated into a universal discourse of raising standards, in which the curriculum is seen as unproblematic and pupil cultures as irrelevant. Insofar as there is a difference with Conservative assimilationism it is in the much more central role that is played in Labour's education thinking by discourses of 'school effectiveness' and 'school improvement'. In *'British Schools for British Citizens'*? (Troyna and Hatcher, 1991) we made some critical comments about their influence on Labour's ability to address issues of racial inequality. Six years later, that influence is much more apparent. School effectiveness/school improvement is bidding to become the dominant discourse in education.

Racism and school effectiveness/improvement

The school effectiveness/school improvement paradigm exemplifies the 'social administration' approach mentioned earlier, and invites what Troyna has called, quoting Dale, 'the interrogation of 'the appropriateness and framing of the problems and questions' (Troyna, 1993: p.37). Stephen Ball speaks of the emergence of 'school effectiveness researchers' and 'management theorists', around whose work

> a new relationship to policy or rather inside policy was being forged. Issues relating to system design, analysis of provision and social justice were now replaced by implementation studies focussed on issues like 'quality', 'evaluation', 'leadership' and 'accountability'. (Ball, 1994)

A recent review of school effectiveness research by some of its leading practitioners confirms the neglect of social justice issues. According to Sammons, Hillman and Mortimore (1995), recent research has actually moved away from an earlier concern with equity towards a more generalised focus on the achievements of all students. The problem is not solely one of research priorities. It also, and more fundamentally, relates to one of the theoretical bases of the school effectiveness paradigm, its reliance on correlational studies. For Brown, Duffield and Riddell, 'the statistical technique of multi-level modelling seems to have lent itself to the conceptual leap that arrives at a model for school effectiveness without any diversion imposed by the troubling task of developing theory' (1995: p.8). Lawrence Angus, in a review article on current school effectiveness literature, notes that

Family background, social class, any notion of context, are typically regarded as 'noise' – as 'outside' background factors which must be controlled for and then stripped away so that the researcher can concentrate on the important domain of school factors.

The school, the process of schooling, the culture of pupils, the nature of community, the society, the economy, are not seen in relation to each other. (1993: p.341)

In consequence, school effectiveness research has little to say about the central issue for understanding the construction of educational inequality: the interaction between pupil cultures and the official culture of the school.

The 'school improvement' movement is motivated by a much more explicit concern for 'educationally disadvantaged' pupils, as the title of a recent collection of case studies, *Success Against the Odds* (National Commission on Education, 1996), suggests. Nevertheless, I would argue that the school improvement movement shares the same underdeveloped conceptualisation of educational inequality as the school effectiveness literature. By way of illustration, I want to examine how two recent books, whose aims are to provide a state-of-the-art picture of the school effectiveness and school improvement traditions and how they can be integrated, address issues of 'race'.

The first book I want to refer to is *Merging Traditions: The Future of Research on School Effectiveness and School Improvement* (Gray, Reynolds, Fitz-Gibbon and Jesson, 1996). In the first chapter the issue of differential school effects for students of different ethnic backgrounds is discussed. The evidence is seen to be inconclusive and more research is called for. Thereafter issues of ethnicity play no further part in the book at all. The second book is *Making Good Schools: Linking school effectiveness and school improvement* (Reynolds *et al*, 1996). The deracialised character of its approach is indicated by the absence of any reference to 'race', ethnicity, or multicultural education in the index. The deliberate separation of school effectiveness from issues of ethnicity and culture is exemplified by the chapter by Bollen (1996). He states that one function of the school can be to foster cultural pluralism. But to do so would entail 'a complicated political debate in which the conflicting interests of ideological, political and economic groups will clash' (p9), and this would make the achievement of consensus unlikely. His solution is to define the concept of the 'effective school' as a 'school-specific organisational concept, fit to be used within the context of many other, wider, cultural concepts and in fact aiming at no more than an effective teaching/learning process' (p10). What he is saying here is that the effectiveness of the teaching and learning process can be divorced from cultures of pupils. He uses the notion of 'school culture', but only to refer to the 'official culture of the school', from which pupil cultures are excluded. In this he is typical of the school effectiveness/improvement literature. For example, in another recent book by two leading 'school improvers', Stoll and Fink (1996) devote a chapter to 'The Power of School Culture', but it is defined entirely in terms of the 'official' culture. The existence of pupil cultures is mentioned but they play no further part in their model.

Teacher cultures and pupil cultures

The failure to recognise that school cultures are the product of the interaction between the 'official' culture and the cultures of pupils is a fundamental theoretical flaw in the school effectiveness/ improvement approach. To reduce the culture of the school to its 'official' culture in fact assumes its *imposition* on the school students. There are two principal interfaces between the two cultural domains: the curriculum; and relations between teachers and pupils. In the school effectiveness/school improvement literature, 'Knowledge and curriculum are generally regarded as unproblematic and it is assumed that students must simply learn them' (Angus, 1993: 343). For example, there is no mention of curriculum content in the twelve key 'effectiveness factors' identified by Mortimore *et al.* (1988) and frequently cited subsequently elsewhere. The advocates of school effectiveness/improvement tend to operate with a universal and passive model of the pupil identical to that which is assumed in the National Curriculum. Richard Johnson identifies the problem with this model as follows:

> the great delusion is that all pupils – black and white, working-class and middle-class, boys and girls – will receive the curriculum in the same way. Actually, it will be read in different ways, according to how pupils are placed in social relationships and culture. (1991: p.78)

A number of studies in the field of 'race' have illuminated the way in which the culture of the school is the product of their interaction. For example, David Gillborn and Tony Sewell in their research studies into how the patterns of interaction between teachers and black school students both derived from and shaped the cultures of both students and teachers, and thus of the school as a whole (Gillborn, 1990; Sewell, 1997).

I have discussed one of Troyna's key concepts, that of deracialisation, and applied it to recent Labour Party policy statements and the school effectiveness/improvement movement on which they draw. But of course the phenomenon to which it points is not confined to 'race' alone; it is part of a wider process of abstraction which applies equally to social class and to gender. Labour's modernisers share the same conception of the pupil as their Conservative counterparts, of whom Ken Jones writes:

> The themes of the modernising tendency...are in an important sense acultural...and its conception of the individual is correspondingly non-concrete. [...] That students differ in what their society has made of them; that the sexual, class or racial prisms through which they view the world affect their attitudes to learning and their conceptions of relevance are not important matters. (1989: p.96-7)

Labour Party policy and the school effectiveness/improvement literature are as 'de-classed' and 'de-gendered' as they are de-racialised. But in the area of 'race', the publication of the recent Ofsted report *Recent Research on the Achievements of Ethnic*

Minority Pupils (Gillborn and Gipps, 1996) could mark a turning-point. If its arguments are taken seriously, it will compel those concerned with low achievement by some ethnic minority groups to engage with causal factors which arise from the interaction of 'official' and pupil cultures. This would entail developing a theoretical understanding of both pupil cultures and the role of the school in reproducing inequalities which has up till now been absent from the school effectiveness/improvement paradigm.

Troyna's interest in pupil cultures is evident in a number of his writings (see for example Troyna and Hatcher, 1992). Here I want to focus on his conception of the role of the school in reproducing racial inequality, and argue that if government policy, and the school effectiveness/improvement movement, is going to address issues of racial inequality, and class and gender inequality too, then there are some useful lessons that can be drawn from Troyna's writings on this question.

The starting point is his critique of the Swann report (DES, 1985), which centred on its failure to acknowledge 'institutional racism' in the school. In Troyna's view, it was guilty of

> a continued avoidance of the question of how the educational system might respond effectively to racist impulses in society at large. The Swann committee circumvented this problem by identifying racism primarily in terms of individual prejudice and by recommending Racism Awareness Training (RAT) as a way of correcting cultural misunderstandings. The notion of institutionalised racism, in contrast, was considered 'confused and confusing' by the committee.... (Troyna and Carrington, 1990: p.79)

For Troyna, the concept of 'institutional racism' had a particular meaning, which Fazal Rizvi discusses in his introduction to *Racism and Education* (Rizvi, 1993). Troyna was very critical of the use of the term to apply to the functioning of a specific institution, such as the school, abstracted from the wider political context, and in particular from the state. He saw 'institutional racism' as a 'bridging concept' between negatively racialised within-school processes and structural racism in the wider society. I will give one example of the usefulness of the concept to current debates. One element in institutional racism which Troyna discussed was teachers' expectations. The school effectiveness/improvement literature also regards low teacher expectations as one of the main mechanisms which account for low pupil achievement. But the school effectiveness/ improvement conceptualisation of 'teacher expectations' is not theoretically informed. It is little more than a circular description: pupils underachieve because teachers have low expectations of them, teachers have low expectations because pupils have low achievement. Its function in the literature becomes exhortatory rather than explanatory; its consequences pupil target-setting, which can be a useful strategy but is not a substitute for a comprehensive theory-rich response to low achievement. Yet there is empirical work in the field of 'race' and education, by Green (1982), Carrington (1983), Tomlinson (1987), Wright (1987), Gillborn (1990) and others, which, as Troyna says, reveals that teachers' professional judgements of pupils are often viewed through the lens of a discriminatory 'racial frame of reference', which provides 'the basis for decision-making: the criteria for differentiation and classification of pupils' in day-to-day interaction (Troyna and Carrington, 1990: p.52). The racial frame of reference does not necessarily or even mainly entail consciously racist beliefs: on the contrary, its effectivity is more likely to be the result of

> teachers' tenacious commitment to the principles of universalism and individualism. Assertions such as 'we treat them all the same' (colour-blind) and 'we respond to the individual needs of our children' (child-centred) constitute professional tenets which are incompatible with policies that are designed to address the needs and interests of an entire group of pupils, defined in terms of their 'race', gender or class. (Troyna and Carrington, 1990: p.51)

Troyna's extension of the concept of deracialisation here, by analogy, to gender and social class is suggestive of the contribution it can make to enriching the school effectiveness/improvement perspective.

The state, LEAs and popular pressure

Another central theme of Troyna's writings concerned the ways in which the state attempts to 'manage' issues of 'race'. Authentic antiracist education, for Troyna, therefore inevitably meant a challenge to racism both within the institution and against the state. In the last chapter of his book *Racism and Education* (1993) he mounted a vigorous defence of this conception of the state attempting to manage and re-produce patterns of inequality, not this time against attacks from the Right, but against the charge from a current on the left who accused him of overestimating the role of the state in relation to 'race'. (See also his response to Stephen Ball's conception of the role of the state in the policy process in education: Hatcher and Troyna, 1994).

> I do argue that antiracist education should be geared towards an understanding of the social and racial formation of the state and how it might be possible to challenge and, ultimately, transform it. But to give primacy to certain socio-political structures in explaining the development and reproduction of racial inequalities is not the same as reductionism. To suggest otherwise is to oversimplify, distort and ignore the variants within Marxist thought. (Troyna, 1993: p.119-120)

For Troyna, the dominance of the state is never uncontested. On the basis of the experiences of antiracist education in the 1980s, he saw the focus of resistance as Local Education Authorities. A number of authorities, almost all Labour-controlled, had taken the lead in developing antiracist education policies in opposition to the thrust of Conservative government policy. The determination to prevent LEAs from playing this role was one of the reasons for the drastic erosion of LEA power in the 1988 Education Act (Troyna and Carrington, 1990: p.112). At first sight there is an obvious parallel between the role that LEAs played in instigating and supporting educational reform in terms of racial equality in the 1980s and the role that many school effectiveness/improvement writers have seen them playing in the 1990s, even before the end of the Conservative government in 1997, in pressuring and supporting 'school improvement'. It is a parallel that Troyna himself drew (Troyna and Vincent, 1995).

However, Troyna's analysis of the role of LEAs in fact contrasts strongly with the way the school effectiveness/improvement litera-ture depicts it. Much of this literature depoliticises the character of local authorities, reducing them to their technical functions at the expense of their 'democratic' ones. Even the recent 'learning society' literature, which has the merit of wanting to enhance the democratic functions of LEAs, tends to present an abstract and idealised model of local government (e.g. Ranson, 1994, Nixon *et al*, 1996, Hatcher, 1996). The strength of Troyna's approach is that it is based on a politically and historically situated understanding of local authorities. This has two elements, inside and outside the local state.

Troyna repeatedly emphasises the role of outside pressure in forcing LEAs to respond to racial inequality. The dynamic for antiracist policies did not come primarily from within local government but from outside, and above all from the black communities themselves. Perhaps the most important starting-point was Bernard Coard's pamphlet *How the West Indian Child is Made Educationally Subnormal in the British School System* (1971). This was not intended as an academic publication but as a popular pamphlet around which numerous public meetings took place in the black community. It was followed in the 1970s by threats of boycotts by the Black Parents' Movement, by action by black school students (e.g. the strike at Tulse Hill school), and by alliances between black and white activists (which led to antiracist policies in Berkshire, for example) (Troyna, 1993: p.31, 50). The pressure was stepped up in the late 1970s by the rise of the National Front (accompanied by a number of racist murders) and the successful mass popular opposition to it by the Anti-Nazi League, Rock Against Racism and similar organisations. In education, the response was the formation of the influential campaigning organisation ALTARF (All-London Teachers Against Racism and Fascism) (Troyna and Carrington, 1990: p.27-32).

The 1980s began with riots involving black youth in Bristol, Brixton and elsewhere. This resulted in further steps by local authorities to develop policies on racial equality, amid a succession of local struggles. The case of the Bradford headteacher Ray Honeyford is well-known; less well-known is the militant character of the community campaign which forced his dismissal, involving demonstrations, pickets and a school boycott. Equally militant was the Campaign Against Racism's campaign for reforms at Daneford School in East London in 1985. After eleven people were arrested on a picket of the Education Offices, over seventy schools took unofficial strike action and over two thousand teachers demonstrated in protest. At William Patten Infant School in North London the staff closed the school for a day to take part with parents in a deputation to the Home Office to protest against the threatened deportation of two Turkish pupils, and later produced a book and a video about the campaign.

Troyna's chronicle of the manifestations of pressure on the local state from without is accompanied by an analysis of the social groups within local authorities (1993: p.31-3). He notes that popular voices tend not to be heard unless taken up by 'policy entrepreneurs' – councillors and officers committed to change and making skilful use of pressure from communities or central agencies. A decisive influence was the emergence of a layer of Labour councillors who, for various reasons, were responsive to demands from the black communities. Troyna also discusses the role of other forces: professional groups such as education officers and the teacher unions, and campaigning education organisations.

The Labour Party in local government always has a Janus-like character, attempting to satisfy the demands of its social base in the local working class while carrying out the requirements of the central state. In the 1980s LEAs were sites of struggle, and Troyna explored their ambivalent stance in his case studies of Manchester and Inner London education authorities (Troyna, 1993). In Manchester the combination of pressure from black organisations and the rise of the National Front led to what Troyna calls a 'control model' of consultation with the black communities. He describes the anti-prejudice policy which ensued in 1980 as a 'cultural understanding' rather than an antiracist model. In ILEA, pressure from black parents concerned with low achievement resulted in a policy of 'benevolent multiculturalism', whose aim was to increase the compatibility of the school culture with that of the home in order to improve achievement. In both cases – and there is another parallel here with the 'school effectiveness/improvement' approach – the local authorities adopted a bipartisan strategy which meant ignoring issues which would undermine it, such as mother tongue support. The justifiability of Troyna's critique of 1980s 'municipal antiracism' has been confirmed by other leading observers. For example, Herman Ouseley speaks of a balance-sheet of failure and a retreat to a colour-blind approach: 'lacking a vision of how to embrace the 'usually excluded' groups of people from their local communities, it has become easier to embrace the survivalist culture and the new realism' (1990: p.150).

Theorising popular agency in educational change

Apart from Troyna's work (and Arnot, 1991), no systematic account of this important period in egalitarian education reform has been attempted. Troyna's analysis of the social forces involved in the development of local authority policy on racial equality in the 1980s is particularly valuable. I want to single out one dimension of Troyna's work, which points to a fundamental weakness in recent and contemporary writing on education, and that is a theorisation of popular social agency. It is noticeably absent from the 'school improvement' vision, which defines the involvement of parents (supporting learning in the home, participating in school activities) and teachers (the 'empowered' teacher in the collegiate school) in individualist terms but makes no space for a more collective and political role. A striking confirmation is the complete disregard of the school improvement movement for one of the most important attempts to improve schools in the 1990s, the national campaign by parents and teachers led by FACE (Fight Against Cuts in Education) to increase spending on schools and reduce class sizes.

This failure by 'school improvers' to address collective agency is shared by educationists on the left, who have, with few exceptions, been equally silent about the collective roles of teachers, parents and others in the politics of education of the past twenty years. They have defined 'resistance' to social reproduction in terms of the responses of pupils, or the stances of individual teachers, but not in terms of organised collective action by teachers (and young people). They have, for example, failed to integrate an analysis of the role of the teachers' unions, from the industrial action of the mid-1980s to the boycotts of tests in the 1990s. They have analysed the 'policy elite', but there is no corresponding exploration of the 'policy poor'. Some have even theorised away altogether the possibility of collective emancipatory action.

Troyna regarded the decisive role played by popular collective agency under a Conservative government in the 1980s in putting pressure on LEAs and government as equally necessary under a Labour government in the 1990s. He noted changes in the role of LEAs, as a result of government legislation. Some were reinventing themselves in accord with a private sector managerialist model, in which 'social justice issues, based on anything other than the most cursory criteria, are silenced' (Troyna and Vincent, 1994: p.32). Others – he suggests Birmingham as an example – were adopting a model of the 'enabling authority' which Stewart Ranson (1992) has identified as having the potential to reverse the thrust of central government's individualist-consumerist ethos and revitalise a conception of 'active citizenship' and collective public choice.

> It is these settings, where the local state demonstrates its con-
> cern to address the issues raised by its heterogeneous com-
> munities that we see the greatest potential for the pursuit of
> social justice issues in education. None of this guarantees that
> Birmingham, or any other LEA for that matter, will subordinate
> its traditional concern with the redistribution of the 'social

good' (i.e. education) to tackling a more ambitious conception of social justice, involving greater and more diverse levels of participation. (Troyna and Vincent, 1994: p.32-3)

Where Troyna differs from the conception of the new model LEA advocated by Ranson and others is his understanding of conflicting public interests in education. As Carol Vincent concludes in her study of parental power and influence,

> whether at school or LEA level, policies are likely to be the focus for conflict and competition. This may mean that 'opposi-tional' policies calling for change to the current balance of power have a relatively small chance of finding their way onto the political agenda (1996: p.157).

This is a different conception from that of Ranson (1994). The case Ranson makes for education as a public service rather than a market-place is powerful, but it assumes the flawed premise that it can be based on consensus. He is right to point out that 'Developments which have become preconditions for the educational progress of many young people – a gender neutral curriculum, bilingual teaching, multicultural education, comprehensive schooling – did not emerge from Whitehall, nor from isolated individuals but instead from local discourse and public action' (Ranson, 1993: p.3), but, as Troyna has consistently demonstrated, there has never been consensus around these goals. Progress towards achieving them, still unfinished, has always been the result of partisan pressure against their opponents. Given the extent to which the new Labour govern-ment has accommodated to the Conservative agenda, progress towards social justice in education will continue to require organised pressure at local and national levels.

From this conception of the inevitably conflictual and partisan character of social agency in educational reform stems Troyna's stance on the role of the education researcher. He placed himself in the tradition of critical social research, which he defined as being 'concerned not only with unpacking reality, but suggesting ways of altering it; to provide genuine support, in other words, in the struggle against the structural oppression of discernible groups' (1994, p.82). A corollary of their failure to theorise collective social agency has been the widespread failure of academics in education to connect with and participate in it. As Michael Apple (1996) points out, the right in education has been rather more successful in producing 'public intellectuals' than the left. In Britain, the new period in the politics of education opened up by the end of the Conservative government offers a new opportunity to build a stronger professional and political alliance between academic educationists and other stakeholders committed to social justice in education. Barry Troyna would have been part of it: through his work he still is.

References

Angus, L. (1993) The Sociology of School Effectiveness, *British Journal of Sociology of Education*, 14, 3, 333-345

Apple, M. (1996) *Cultural Politics and Education,* Buckingham, Open University Press

Arnot, M. (1991) Equality and Democracy: A Decade of Struggle Over Education, *British Journal of Sociology of Education*, 12, 4, 447-466

Ball, S. (1988) Comprehensive Schooling, Effectiveness and Control: An Analysis of Educational Discourses. In Slee, R. (Ed.) *Discipline and Schools,* London, Macmillan

Ball, S.J. (1994) Intellectuals or Technicians: The Urgent Role of Theory in Educational Studies. Annual Address to the Standing Conference for Studies in Education, Royal Society of Arts, London, 4 November

Bollen, R. (1996) School Effectiveness and School Improvement: The Intellectual and Policy Context, In Reynolds, D., Bollen, R., Creemers, B., Hopkins, D., Stoll, L. and Lagerweij, N. (Eds.) *Making Good Schools: Linking school effectiveness and school improvement,* London, Routledge

Brown, S., Duffield, J. and Riddell, S. (1995) School Effectiveness Research: The Policy Makers' Tool for School Improvement? *EERA Bulletin*, March, 6-15

Carrington, B. (1983) Sport As A Side-Track: An Analysis of West Indian Involvement in Sport, In Barton, L. and Walker, S. (Eds.) *Race, Class and Education,* London, Croom Helm

Coard, B. (1971) *How the West Indian Child is Made Educationally Subnormal in the British School System,* London, New Beacon

Dale, R. (1986) *Introducing Education Policy: Principles and Perspectives,* Milton Keynes, Open University Press

Department of Education and Science (1985) *Education for All* (the Swann Report), London, HMSO

Gillborn, D. (1990) *'Race', Ethnicity and Education,* London, Unwin Hyman

Gillborn, D. and Gipps, C. (1996) *Recent Research on the Achievements of Ethnic Minority Pupils,* London, HMSO

Gray, J., Reynolds, D., Fitz-Gibbon, C. and Jesson, D. (Eds.) (1996) *Merging Traditions: The Future of Research on School Effectiveness and School Improvement,* London, Cassell

Green, P.A. (1982) 'Teachers' Influence on the Self-Concept of Pupils of Different Ethnic Groups', Unpublished PhD thesis, University of Durham

Hatcher, R. (1996) 'The Limitations of the New Social-Democratic Agendas: Class, Equality and Agency', Hatcher, R. and Jones, K. (Eds.) *Education after the Conservatives,* Stoke-on-Trent, Trentham

Hatcher, R. and Troyna, B. (1994) 'The 'Policy Cycle': A Ball by Ball Account', *Journal of Education Policy,* 9, 2, 155-170

Johnson, R. (1991) *'A New Road to Serfdom? A Critical History of the 1988 Act',* London, Unwin Hyman

Jones, K. (1989) *Right Turn,* London, Hutchinson

The Labour Party (1989a) *Multicultural Education: Labour's Policy for Schools,* London, Labour Party

The Labour Party (1989b) *Policy Review: Good Education For All,* London, Labour Party

The Labour Party (1989c) *Children First: Labour's Policy for Raising Standards in Schools,* London, Labour Party

The Labour Party (1994) *Opening doors to a learning society,* London, Labour Party

The Labour Party (1995) *Excellence For Everyone,* London, Labour Party

Miles, R. (1988) 'Racialisation'. In Cashmore, E. (Ed.) *Dictionary of Race and Ethnic Relations (2nd edition),* London, Routledge

Mortimore. P., Sammons, P., Stoll, L., Lewis, D. and Ecob, R. (1988) *School Matters,* Wells, Open Books

National Commission on Education (1996) *Success Against the Odds,* London, Routledge

Nixon, J., Martin, J., McKeown, P. and Ranson, S. (1996) *Encouraging Learning: Towards a Theory of the Learning School,* Buckingham, Open University Press

Ouseley, H. (1990) 'Resisting Institutional Change' in Ball, W. and Solomos, J. (Eds.) *Race and Local Politics,* Basingstoke, Macmillan

Ranson, S. (1992) *The Role of Local Government in Education,* London, Longman

Ranson, S. (1993) *Local Democracy for the Learning Society,* National Commission on Education Briefing No. 18. London, National Commission on Education

Ranson, S. (1994) *Towards the Learning Society,* London, Cassell

Reeves, F. (1983) *British Racial Discourse,* Cambridge, Cambridge University Press

Reynolds, D., Bollen, R., Creemers, B., Hopkins, D., Stoll, L. and Lagerweij, N. (1996) *Making Good Schools: Linking school effectiveness and school improvement,* London, Routledge

Rizvi, F. (1993) 'Critical Introduction: Researching Racism and Education'. In Troyna, B., *Racism and Education,* Milton Keynes, Open University Press

Sammons, P., Hillman, J. and Mortimore, P. (1995) *Key Characteristics of Effective Schools: A Review of School Effectiveness Research,* London, Institute of Education/Ofsted

Sewell, T. (1997) *Black Masculinities and Schooling,* Stoke-on-Trent, Trentham

Stoll, L. and Fink, D. (1996) *Changing Our Schools,* Buckingham, Open University Press

Tomlinson, S. (1987) 'Curriculum Option Choices in Multi-Ethnic Schools'. In Troyna, B. (Ed.) *Racial Equality in Education,* London, Tavistock

Troyna, B. (1993) *Racism and Education,* Buckingham, Open University Press

Troyna, B. (1994) 'Critical Social Research and Education Policy', *British Journal of Education Studies,* 42, 1, 70-84

Troyna, B. and Carrington, B. (1990) *Education, Racism and Reform,* London, Routledge

Troyna, B. and Hatcher, R. (1991) 'British Schools for British Citizens'? *Oxford Review of Education,* 17, 3, 287-299

Troyna, B. and Hatcher, R. (1992) *Racism in Children's Lives,* London, Routledge

Troyna, B. and Vincent, C. (1995) 'The Discourses of Social Justice in Education', *Discourse,* 16, 2, 149-166

Vincent, C. (1996) *Parents and Teachers: Power and Participation,* London, Falmer

Wright, C. (1987) 'Black Students – White Teachers'. In Troyna, B. (Ed.) *Racial Equality and Education,* London, Tavistock

List of Contributors

Dr Pat Sikes – Warwick Institute of Education, University of Warwick.

Professor Fazal Rizvi – School of Graduate Studies, Faculty of Education, Monash University.

Dr Carol Vincent – Warwick Institute of Education, University of Warwick.

Professor Sally Tomlinson – Department of Educational Studies, Goldsmith's College, University of London.

Professor David Halpin – Department of Eductional Studies, Goldsmith's College, University of London.

Professor Jean Rudduck – Homerton College, Cambridge.

Professor Gaby Weiner – South Bank University, London.

Sandra Shipton – Headteacher, Edgewick Community Primary School, Coventry.

Professor Ivor Goodson – Centre for Applied Research in Education, University of East Anglia, Norwich and Warner Graduate School, University of Rochester, Rochester.

Dr Vicki Crowley – Department of Communications and Information Studies, University of South Australia.

Dr Roger Dale – Department of Education, University of Auckland.

Dr Bob Lingard – Graduate School of Education, University of Queensland.

Prof John Rex – Professor Emeritus, Centre for Research in Ethnic Relations, University of Warwick.

Dr Richard Hatcher – Faculty of Education, University of Central England, Birmingham.

BARRY TROYNA'S PUBLICATIONS

1977   'Reggae: An Annotated Bibliography', *Community
        Relations Commission (CRC) Journal,* Vol.5, February
        pp.36-37

1977   'The Reggae War' *New Society* 10th March.
        Reprinted *in Race and Immigration,* (2nd Edition), A
        New Society Social Studies Reader, London, International
        Publishing Corporation, pp. 491-492

1977   'The Rastafarians: The Youths' Response', *Multiracial
        School,* Vol.6, No.1. pp.1-9

1977   'Angry Youngsters – A Response to Racism in Britain', *Youth
        in Society,* No.26, December pp. 13-15

1978   'Black and Bitter', *Youth in Society* No.29, June (with Colin
        Lago) pp.17-19

1978   'Racism and the Radical Right: A Review Essay', *New
        Approaches in Multiracial Education,* Vol.7, No.3. pp.14-15

1978   *Rastafarianism, Reggae and Racism,* National Association for
        Multiracial Education

1978   'Race and Streaming: A Case Study', *Educational Review,*
        Vol.30, No.1. pp.59-65

1979   'Differential Commitment to Ethnic Identity by Black Youths
        in Britain', *New Community,* Vol.7, No.3. pp.406-415

1979   'What Could the BBC Do About the NF?', *Broadcast* 30th
        April, (with Mike Tracey) pp. 30-32

1980   'The Media and the Electoral Decline of the National Front',
        Patterns of Prejudice, Vol.14, No.3. pp.25-31

1981   'Watching the World Go By: The Effects of Mass Media on Childrens' Attitudes to Foreign Countries', *The New Era,* No.4, (with Virginia Nightingale) pp.126-130.

1981   'Recruiting Racists', *Youth in Society,* No.60, (with Graham Murdock) pp.8-11

1981   'Just for White Boys? Elitism, Racism and Research', *Multiracial Education,* Vol.10, No.1, (with Ernest Cashmore). pp.27-31

1981   *Public Awareness and the Media: A Study of Reporting on Race,* London, Commission for Racial Equality

1982   *Black Youth in Crisis,* London, Allen and Unwin (Co-edited with E.E. Cashmore)

1982   'Racial Antipathy and Local Opinion Leaders: A Tale of Two Cities', *New Community,* Vol. 9, No.3, (with Robin Ward). pp.454-466

1982   'Multiracial Education and the Politics of Decision-Making', *Oxford Review of Education*, Vol.8, No.2, (with Andrew Dorn) pp.175-186

1982   'The Ideological and Policy Response to Black Pupils in British Schools', in Anthony Hartnett (Ed.) *The Social Sciences in Educational Studies,* London, Heinemann. Reprinted in R. Burgess (Ed.), *Education, Schools and Schooling,* London, Macmillan, 1985. pp.127-143

1982   'Reporting the National Front: British Values Observed' in Charles Husband (Ed.) *'Race' in Britain: Continuity and Change,* London, Hutchinson. pp.259-278

1982   'Growing Up in Babylon' in Cashmore and Troyna (Eds.) *Black Youth in Crisis,* London, Allen and Unwin, (with E.E. Cashmore) pp.72-86

1983   'Educational Myths, Labour Market Realities' in B. Troyna and D. Smith (Eds.) *Racism, School and the Labour Market,* Leicester, National Youth Bureau pp.5-16

1983   *Racism, School and the Labour Market,* Leicester, National
            Youth Bureau (Co-edited with Douglas Smith)

1983   *Introduction to Race Relations,* London, Routledge and Kegan
            Paul (with E. Cashmore)

1983   'Multicultural Education Policies: Are They Worth the Paper
            They're Written on?' *Times Educational Supplement*
            9 December (with Wendy Ball) p.20

1983   'Multiracial Education: Just Another Brick in the Wall?', *New
            Community,* Vol.10, No.3. pp.424-428

1983   'Fascism: Slogan or Concept?', *Patterns of Prejudice,* Vol.17,
            No.4, (with Christopher Dandeker) pp.19-30

1984   'Fact or Artefact: The 'Educational Under-achievement' of
            Black Pupils in British Schools', *British Journal of Sociology
            of Education,* Vol.5, No.2. pp.153-166

1984   'Policy Entrepreneuers' and the Development of LEA Multi
            Ethnic Education Policies: A Reconstruction', *Educational
            Management and Administration,* Vol.12, No.3. (Reprinted
            1986 in Warwick University Reprint Papers in Ethnic
            Relations) pp.203-215

1984   *The Development of Multiethnic, Multicultural Education
            Policies in Four LEAs,* Warwick Working Papers on Ethnic
            Relations (with J. Rex and M. Naguib)

1984   'Multicultural Education: Emancipation or Containment?' in
            L. Barton and S. Walker (Eds.) *Social Crisis and Educational
            Research,* London, Croom Helm pp.75-97

1984   20 Contributions to E.E. Cashmore (Ed.) *A Dictionary of
            Ethnic and Race Relations,* London, Routledge and Kegan
            Paul

1984   'The Product Being Sold is Racial Harmony': A Case Sudy
            in Race Relations and Social Advertising', *Multiracial
            Education* Vol.12, No.2. pp.24-33

1984   'Multicultural Education Policies in Practice', *The Runnymede
            Trust Race and Immigration Bulletin,* No.166 (with
            Wendy Ball) pp.7-15

1985   'Innovating Antiracist Education in Predominantly White Schools', *Perspectives 22,* School of Education, Exeter University pp.44-52

1985   'Crummy' Schools', *Times Educational Supplement,* 27 September p.24

1985   'The 'Racialisation' of Contemporary Education Policy: Its Origins, Nature and Impact in a Period of Contraction' in G. Walford (Ed.) *Schooling in Turmoil,* London, Croom Helm pp.38-58

1985   *Views from the Chalk Face: School Responses to an LEA's Multicultural Education Policy,* Warwick Policy Papers in Ethnic Relations (with Wendy Ball) 2nd Edition, 1987

1985   'Styles of LEA Policy Intervention in Multicultural/Antiracist Education', *Educational Review,* Vol.37, No.2. (with Wendy Ball) pp.165-173

1985   'The Great Divide: Policies and Practice in Multicultural Education', *British Journal of Sociology of Education,* Vol.6, No.2. pp.209-224

1985   'Educational Decision Making and Issues of 'Race': A Study of Policy and Practice on Multicultural Education in a Local Education Authority' *The Quarterly Journal of Social Affairs,* (with Wendy Ball), Vol.1, No.4. pp.311-325

1986   'Swann's Song': The Origins, Ideology and Implications of Educational For All', *Journal of Education Policy* Vol.1, No.2, (Reprinted in T. Chivers (Ed.) *Race and Culture in Education,* Slough, NFER-Nelson, 1987) pp.171-182

1986   *Racism, Education and the State: The Racialisation of Education Policy,* London, Croom Helm (with Jenny Williams)

1986   *'Policy Entrepreneurs' and the Development of Multiethnic Education Policies: A Reconstruction,* Warwick Reprint Papers in Ethnic Relations

1986   'The Controversy Surrounding Raymond Honeyford', *Social Studies Review,* Vol.1, No.4, pp.19-22

1986   'Partnerships, Consultation and Influence: State Rhetoric in the
        Struggle for Racial Equality' in A. Hartnett and M. Naish
        (Eds). *Education and Society Today,* London, Falmer, (with
        Wendy Ball) pp.37-46

1986   'Race, Power, Prejudice' in L. Cohen and A.Cohen (eds)
        Multicultural Education: A Source book for Teachers, New
        York, Harper Row (with E.E. Cashmore) pp.187-205

1987   'A Conceptual Overview of Strategies to Combat Inequality in
        Education: Introductory Essay' in B. Troyna (Ed.) *Racial
        Inequality in Education,* London, Tavistock pp.1-10

1987   'Reporting Racism' in C. Husband (Ed.) *'Race' in Britain:
        Continuity and Change (2nd Edition),* London, Hutchinson.
        pp. 275-291

1987   *Conceptual and Strategic Approaches to Race-Related Matters
        in Educational Policymaking* (Occasional Paper No.4), Centre
        for Race and Ethnic Studies, Free University of Amsterdam

1987   *Racial Inequality in Education,* (Ed.) London, Tavistock.
        (Reprinted in 1989)

1987   'Antisexist/Antiracist Education – A False Dilemma: A Reply
        to Walking and Brannigan', *Journal of Moral Education,*
        Vol.16, No.1 (with Bruce Carrington) pp.60-65

1987   'Resistance, Rights and Rituals: Denominational Schools and
        Multicultural Education' *Journal of Education Policy,* Vol.2,
        No.1 (with Wendy Ball) pp.15-25 Reprinted in 1993 in L.J.
        Francis and D. Lankshear (Eds.) *Christian Perspectives on
        Church Schools,* London, Fowler Wright.

1987   'Beyond Multiculturalism: Towards the Enactment of Anti-
        racist Education in Policy, Provision and Pedagogy', *Oxford
        Review of Education,* Vol.13, No.3. (Reprinted in S. Allen and
        M. Macey (Eds.) *Race and Social Policy,* London, ESRC
        (1988)) pp.307-320

1988   'Conceptual and Ethical Dilemmas of Collaborative Research:
        Reflections on a Case Study', *Educational Review,* Vol.40,
        No.3 (with Peter Foster) pp.289-300

1988   'Paradigm Regained: a Critique of 'Cultural Deficit' Theories in Contemporary Educational Research', *Comparative Education,* Vol.24, No.3 pp.273-284

1988   'Rethinking 'Equality of Opportunity' in Education' *Critical Social Policy,* 23, Autumn pp.119-122

1988   *Children and Controversial Issues: Strategies for the Early and Middle Years of Schooling,* London, Falmer, Co-editor with Bruce Carrington

1988   'Swann – three years on', *Education,* 8 April, p.298

1988   'Selection' and 'Learning': Frameworks for Antiracist Initiatives in Education', *Multicultural Teaching,* Vol.6, No.3 pp.5-7

1988   'British Schooling and the Reproduction of Racial Inequality' in M. Cross and H. Entzinger (Eds.) *Lost Illusions,* London, Tavistock pp.186-203

1988   'The Career of an Antiracist Education School Policy: Some Observations On the Mismanagement of Change' in T. Green and S. Ball (Eds.) *Progress and Inequality in Comprehensive Education,* London, Routledge pp.173-192

1988   'Combating Racism through Political Education' in B. Carrington and B. Troyna (Eds.) *Children and Controversial Issues,* London, Falmer pp.205-222

1988   'Race' and Education in the UK' in E.E. Cashmore (Ed.) *Dictionary of Race and Ethnic Relations,* (2nd Edition) London, Routledge

1988   'Teacher Education in the Council of Europe', *European Workshop on Multicultural Studies in Higher Education,* Strasbourg Council of Europe pp.17-28

1989   'A New Planet'? Tackling Racial Inequality in All-White Schools and Colleges' in G. Verma (Ed.) *Education For All: A Landmark in Pluralism,* London, Falmer pp.175-191

1989   'The Dawn of a New ERA? The Education Reform Act, 'Race' and LEAs', *Educational Management and Administration,* Vol.17, No. 1 (with Wendy Ball) pp.23-31

1989   'Surviving in the 'Survivalist Culture': Antiracist Strategies and Practice in the New ERA', *Journal of Further and Higher Education,* Vol.13, No.2 (with Libby Selman) pp.22-36

1989   'Putting the 'Why' Back Into Teacher Education', *Forum,* Vol.32, No.1, (with Pat Sikes) pp.25-27

1989   'Whose Side are We On?' Ethical Dilemmas in Research on 'Race' and Education' in R.G. Burgess (Ed.) *The Ethics of Educational Research,* London, Falmer (with B. Carrington) pp.205-223

1990   'Pragmatism or Retreat? Funding Policy, Local Government and the Marginalisation of Antiracist Education' in W. Ball and J. Solomos (Eds.) *Race and Local Politics,* London, Macmillan (with W. Ball and B. Gulam) pp.78-94

1990   *Racism, Education and Reform,* London, Routledge (with B. Carrington)

1990   *Introduction to Race Relations: Second Edition,* London, Falmer (with E. Cashmore)

1990   'Reform or Deform? The 1988 Education Reform Act and Racial Equality in Britain', *New Community,* Vol.16, No.2. pp.403-417

1991   'True Stories: A Case Study in the Use of Life History in Initial Teacher Education', *Education Review* (with Pat Sikes) Vol.43, No.1 pp.3-16

1991   'Racist Incidents in Schools: A Framework for Analysis' *Journal of Education Policy* (with R. Hatcher) Vol.6, No.1. (Reprinted in D. Gill, *et al* (Eds.) *Racism and Education: Structures and Strategies,* London, Sage pp.17-31

1991   'British Schools for British Citizens?', *Oxford Review of Education,* Vol.17, No.3 (with R. Hatcher) pp.287-299

1991   'Children, 'Race' and Racism: The Limitations of Research
            and Policy', *British Journal of Educational Studies,* Vol.39,
            No.4, pp.425-436

1991   'Underachievers or Under-rated? The Experiences of Pupils of
            South Asian Origin in a Secondary School', *British
            Educational Research Journal,* Vol.17, No.4, pp.361-376

1991   *Multicultural and Antiracist Education in Mainly White
            Colleges,* London, Further Education Unit (with Libby
            Selman)

1991   'Science for All? Antiracism, Science and the Primary School'
            in A. Peacock (Ed.) *Science in Primary Schools: The
            Multicultural Dimension,* London, Macmillan (with S. Farrow)
            pp.63-77

1992   'Can You See The Join? An Historical Analysis of
            Multicultural and Antiracist Education Policies' in D. Gill, *et
            al.* (Eds.) *Racism and Education: Structure and Strategies,*
            London, Sage pp.63-91

1992   *Racism in Children's Lives,* London, Routledge (with R.
            Hatcher)

1992   'Names Can Always Hurt Me', *Times Educational
            Supplement,* 24 January (with R. Hatcher) p.27

1992   'Ethnicity and The Organisation of Learning Groups: A Case
            Study', *Educational Research* Vol.34, No.1, pp.45-56

1992   'It's Only Words: Understanding 'Racial' and Racist
            Incidents', *New Community,* Vol.18, No.3, (with Richard
            Hatcher) pp.493-496

1992   'Education Report', *New Community,* Vol.19, No.1, pp.143-
            147

1993   'Providing Support or Denying Access? The Experiences of
            Students Designated 'ESL' or 'SN' in a Multi-ethnic
            Secondary School', *Educational Review,* (with I. Siraj-
            Blatchford) Vol.45, No.1, pp. 3-11

1993   'Underachievers' or Misunderstood? A Reply to Roger
            Gomm', *British Educational Research Journal,* Vol.19, No.2,
            pp.167-174

1993   'Equal Opportunities, Research and Educational Reform:
Some Introductory Notes', *British Educational Research
Journal,* Vol.19, No.3 (with I. Siraj-Blatchford) pp. 223-226

1993   'Racialisation and Children' in W. Crichlow and C. McCarthy
(eds). *Race, Identity and Representation in Education,*
London, Routledge (with R. Hatcher) pp. 109-125

1993   'Using Students' Own Life Histories' in Sociology Teaching
Handbook Group (Eds.) *Sociology Teaching Handbook,*
Sheffield, University of Sheffield (with Pat Sikes)

1993   *Racism and Education: Research Perspectives* (Modern
Educational Thought series) Milton Keynes, Open University
Press

1993   *The Educational Needs of a Multiracial Society,* Warwick
Occasional Papers in Ethnic Relations (with V. Edwards)

1994   *Local Management of Schools and Racial Equality,* London,
Commission for Racial Equality (with R. Hatcher and D.
Gewirtz)

1994   'Policy Studies Have Come Of Age', *Times Higher
Educational Supplement,* (with D. Halpin), 25 November, p.14

1994   *Dictionary of Race and Ethnic Relations: Third Edition,*
London, Routledge (Co-author)

1994   'Reforms, Research and Being Reflexive About Being
Reflective' in D. Halpin and B. Troyna (Eds) *Researching
Education Policy: Ethical and Methodological Issues,* London,
Falmer, pp. 1-14.

1994   *Researching Education Policy: Ethical and Methodological
Issues,* London, Falmer (Co-editor with David Halpin)

1994   'Critical Social Research and Education Policy', *British
Journal of Educational Studies,* Vol.42, No.1, pp. 70-84

1994   'The 'Policy Cycle': A Ball by Ball account', *Journal of
Education Policy*, Vol.9, No.2 (with R. Hatcher), pp. 155-170

1994   'Blind Faith? Empowerment and Educational Research',
        International Studies in Sociology of Education, Vol.4, No.1,
        pp.3-24

1994   'The 'Everyday World' of Teachers? Deracialised Discourses
        in the Sociology of Teachers and the Teaching Profession',
        British Journal of Sociology of Education, Vol.15, No.3, pp.
        325-339

1995   'The Discourses of Social Justice in Education', *Discourse:
        Studies in the Cultural Politics of Education,* Vol.16, No.2,
        (with C. Vincent) pp.149-166

1995   'The Politics of 'Policy Borrowing', *Comparative Education,*
        Vol.31, No.3 (with D. Halpin)

1995   'Beyond Reasonable Doubt: Researching 'Race' in
        Educational Settings', *Oxford Review of Education,* Vol.21,
        No.4.

1995   *Antiracism, Culture and Social Justice in Education*
        (with Morwenna Griffiths) Stoke on Trent, Trentham
        (Co-editor)

1995   'Local Management of Schools and Racial Equality in
        Education' in S. Tomlinson and M. Craft (Eds.) *Ethnic
        Relations in Schooling: Policy and Practice for the 1990s,*
        Athlone Press, pp. 140-154.

1996   'Minorities' in J.J. Chambliss *et al* (Eds.) *Philosophy of
        Education: An Encyclopedia,* London: Garland

1996   'The Ideology of Expertism: The Framing Of Special
        Education and Racial Equality Policies in the Local State' in C.
        Christensen *et al* (Eds.) *Disability and the Dilemmas of
        Education and Justice,* Milton Keynes, Open University Press
        (with C. Vincent)

1996   *Racial Equality and the Local Management of Schools,* Stoke
        on Trent, Trentham (with R. Hatcher and D. Gewirtz)

Forthcoming: *Research 'Race' in Educational Settings* (Open University
Press) Co-editor with Paul Connolly

Forthcoming: Series Editor *Doing Qualitative Research in Educational
Settings* (Open University Press) Co-editor